SOME IMPORTANT AREAS COVERED:

- Attaining the goals of mutual love, trust, and commitment
- Combating inner loneliness
- Overcoming crises
- The place of sex
- Effective family planning, including adoption and birth control

AND ESPECIALLY FOR YOUNG PEOPLE:

- How to tell the difference between love and infatuation
- The role of dating
- Petting—right or wrong?
- The engagement period

An important, pertinent, relevant book for all who plan on marriage, will be married, or who plan on staying married!

DESIGN FOR CHRISTIAN MARRIAGE

DWIGHT HERVEY SMALL

SPIRE BOOKS

SPIRE BOOKS • Old Tappan, New Jersey

Scripture quotations designated RSV are from the Revised Standard Version of the Bible, copyrighted 1946 and 1952. Those designated ASV are from the American Standard Version.

DESIGN FOR CHRISTIAN MARRIAGE

A SPIRE BOOK
Published by Pyramid Publications for Fleming H. Revell Co.

Spire edition published June, 1971
   Fifth printing June, 1976

Copyright © MCMLIX, by Fleming H. Revell Company

All Rights Reserved

Library of Congress Catalog Card Number: 59-5498

Printed in the United States of America

SPIRE BOOKS are published by Fleming H. Revell Company
Old Tappan, New Jersey 07675, U.S.A.

To the three women in my life:

MY WIFE, RUTH
MY DAUGHTERS, LYNNE AND SHARON

Teachers three!

CONTENTS

FOREWORD

THIS BOOK ATTEMPTS TO trace modern marriage from quest to inquest. That is, it explores the territory from casual dating to the prevalent causes for marital break-up. It is the thesis of this book that Christian marriage is unique, that it is truly creative, and that it is inherently fortified against such pathological deterioration as leads to divorce. Christian marriage is more than a lofty concept that provides an unattainable ideal; it is a dynamic relationship that links the very power of God to the marriage union.

No adequate experience of the completely shared life can avoid certain disappointment and disillusionment. Full personal intimacy in marriage will invariably bring to it certain conflict and tension. This critical problem is enormously accentuated in our time as the result of three relentless trends in our culture. First is that of a highly mechanized pattern of life brought about by industrialization. Second is that of urbanization, the collecting of masses of our population into the great cities where personal anonymity is unavoidable and where social stresses are multiplied. Third is that of the rapidly increasing mobility of neighborhoods, diminishing the sense of community and the possibilities of inter-family relations of a permanent and vitally enriching nature. Individuals are more and more compelled to seek their experience of personal intimacy within their marriage and family. Counteracting the values of such intimacy within the marriage and family relation are the stresses and conflicts which such intimacy creates. Deepening personal intimacy within marriage develops its own kind of conflict of values, and this conflict within the very love relation threatens to destroy that love. Exposed in its true nature is the inherent tragedy of all human love. The conflict is brought about by self-devotion and the inadequate capacity of persons for mutual love, trust, and fidelity. The pathology of marriage must be a serious concern in the face of mounting divorce statistics. Marriage counselling centers and pastors are sounding an urgent alarm. And the more appalling picture still is of those countless numbers who have not divorced, but are living a lie, whose marriage is only an empty shell, a grotesque caricature of the real thing. Disillusioned and apathetic, a seeming majority do little to remedy the situation. Indeed few seem to know where to turn for help. Only a small part of the total tragedy can be pieced together from the available data.

It has been noted that people would not get divorced for such trivial reasons if they did not get married for such trivial reasons! The forces of sociology and psychology are now well marshaled in the campaign for marriage education, and gratifying strides are being made. But the disintegration has not yet begun to diminish. While over two thousand professors in more than six hundred colleges in America are teaching marriage courses and producing substantial research and textbook materials, it is only within the past ten years or so that Christian colleges have seriously undertaken to offer such courses, and these have not generally been taught by full professors of sociology or psychology. To the writer's knowledge there is not one full-length textbook of college calibre that has been issued by an evangelical Christian trained in this field.

It is to Christian theology that we must turn for our keenest insights and hardiest solutions. The goal ahead is creative Christian marriage, where a realistic approach to the conflicts of intimacy and the clash of values arising from self-devoted persons paves the way toward dynamic spiritual solutions. Neither marital breakup nor loveless coexistence finds any place in the Christian scheme of marriage. In an experience of redemptive love and a personal relation to Christ, these very conflicts and tensions may become instruments for fulfillment. It is possible to live out joyously a completely shared life within the boundaries of Christian marriage. The spiritual dimension makes the difference. Here is the way to fulfill complete mutual love, trust, and fidelity!

To the committed Christian couple, marriage can be no less than a three-dimensional thing. A Christian is such because Christ is at the center of his life; a Christian marriage is such because Christ is at the center of it too. And whenever Christ is at the center of a human relationship, there must of necessity be a redemptive experience of His love and grace. He brings a vital quality into every area of human experience, transforming every troubled segment of the relationship, and transcending every human inadequacy. Personal union with Christ is not the way out, but the way through!

Emotional immaturity lies at the heart of marital impasse. At least this is the label attached by the authorities. To a large extent emotional immaturity is related to spiritual immaturity. Insofar as this is discovered to be the case, spiritual roots are important and cannot be ignored. Emotional maturity will engender emotional unity between a married couple, and in precisely the same way spiritual maturity will engender spiritual unity. If there is no spiritual oneness in a marriage, the deepest hungers will not be met, the deepest resources will not be tapped, and the deepest relations will not be cemented. Christian marriage offers the way to real oneness by pointing to a unifying center and power outside of the couple themselves. This oneness is not a mere elusive idealism. It is rather the exciting possibility before every couple that is committed to the Lordship of Christ over all of their life together.

Sexual sanctity can easily be soiled outside of marriage; it can also be shopworn within marriage. The true nature and purpose of the sexual union can just as seriously be mismanaged inside of marriage as outside. Simply to keep sex for marriage is not sufficient to make it immune from tragedy and betrayal. Sex can be a sacrament or a sacrilege right within the marriage relation. It can be a hallowed thing or a hollow thing, a blessing or a burden. It is either a physical act from which there emerges a spiritual value, or it is a physical act and no more. Either it brings a deep sense of mutuality and oneness in love and trust, or it stands alone as a symbol of the ease with which two persons can exploit a pleasurable experience for purely selfish ends. It exalts and dignifies human personality, or it degrades the sacred worth of personality. It is a fine line that separates between the sexual expression of love and the sexual expression of contempt. Lust is not ever far from love in human experience. Only Christian marriage fully guarantees the redemption of sexual expression from the realm of lust. Sexual sanctions for the Christian are guarded by high and holy purposes. The design of this book is to trace the order of God as against the disorder of man.

Successful marriage is the achievement of time and labor. Marriage is not a romantic experience; it is the commitment of two persons to the working out of life together. Marriage is far less concerned with the "She's perfect!" stage, and far more with the realities represented in the husband's exclamation: "Dear, I got a raise! Now we can afford last year's taxes!"

The problems antecedent to marriage deserve a real hearing. The transition from casual dating into courtship is perhaps one of the most confusing periods of life, if for no other reason than that it occurs during adolescence. The emotional and social rigors of these days are not such as many adults would care to repeat.

Is petting wise or otherwise? How does one distinguish that old black magic of romantic infatuation from the real thing called love? Are short engagements prophetic of short marriages? On what basis does a Christian choose a life mate? How much may be expected from the sexual side of marriage? How far can forgiveness go in offenses against the ideal of marriage? These and many other questions must be pondered at least.

A good deal of psychological analysis enters into these pages, and that for the reason that one must have insight into the nature of these mysterious intangibles called love, sex, and marriage before one can organize a tactical approach to his own needs. The end, however, is a very practical one. May the effort of reading these pages be part of the rewarding effort which is necessary to achieve the kind of marriage every Christian young person dreams about.

For fifteen years the subject matter of this book has been part of the author's daily life as a pastor-counsellor. It has been tested in the marriages of several hundred young couples. It has been the working hypothesis in the salvaging of not a few badly damaged marriages. But perhaps of greater significance still, this same material has passed through the clinical testing of a college classroom. With some revision and expansion, these chapters reproduce the lectures given in the Marriage and Family course at Wheaton College. Seniors in Sociology have contributed greatly to the value of the material by their probing questions during discussion periods. Their own experience and research is clearly woven into the fabric of these chapters. To the consecrated young people in one of America's most outstanding Christian colleges a debt of gratitude is hereby acknowledged.

One further word of acknowledgment and appreciation is necessary. A personal friend whose encouragement and insights have been a source of inspiration in bringing this material to publication is Dr. William H. Whiteley, neurosurgeon and Professor of neurosurgery at Jefferson Medical College in Philadelphia, and one of the founding and guiding figures in the Christian Medical Society. His insights in the field of Christian marriage counselling have helped shape the author's point of view.

Many subjects vital to successful marriage are not touched upon here. The physiology and technique of the sexual relation are not discussed, although admittedly nothing could be more crucial to marriage success. Other volumes treat these subjects thoroughly. This and other deficiencies in subject treatment may be alleviated somewhat by the following consideration. All behavior issues from two sources: the concepts that are formed through the years, and the compulsions which make up the emotional baggage of the years. Christian idealism, if taken seriously, will lead to Christian motivation. True Christian commitment is rewarded by the incoming power of the Holy Spirit to guide and enable a conscientious individual in the fulfillment of his idealism. The task tackled in this book is to set forth the Biblical basis for love and marriage, and thus to provide a suggested foundation upon which to pray and to work out a creative Christian marriage.

PART I

CONCEPTS OF
CHRISTIAN MARRIAGE

1. CATCHING SIGHT OF THE GOAL

SOCRATES reportedly told his students: "By all means marry. If you get a good wife, twice blessed will you be. If you get a bad wife, you will become a philosopher!" It would seem then that marriage is a good risk come what may. But this is hardly the universal opinion of our day. It is not popular opinion which concerns us, however, but the Christian ideal as set forth in the Holy Scriptures.

Western wisdom since the time of Socrates accepts as a part of social organization that it is necessary to know what is right before one can know what is wrong. It is on this principle that we shall be concerned primarily to ask whether God has a blueprint for marriage. Only as we know God's design can we evaluate what man has made of marriage.

We must necessarily approach the subject with a sense of awe. We are entering into the realms of the sacred and sublime, for marriage is an institution of God. We approach it knowing that no single individual can possibly have all the insights requisite to a full understanding of such a lofty theme. In this connection one cannot but be reminded of the statement of Lord Shaftsbury: "If the Pope had been married, he would never have thought up such a dogma as papal infallibility!"

There is much that can be said and much that needs to be said, though strangely the Christian implications of love, sex, and marriage seem hardly front-page news even in our day when, of all the social problems pressing for solutions, marriage is still number one on the hit parade. There seems to be ample room for some fresh thinking and vital discussion of the reasons why Christian people marry and the purposes they should have in view.

We approach the subject with awe for another reason. In every marriage the inherent dangers are great and the privileges colossal. The gamble is for high stakes, and the game is played for keeps. Imagine the miracle of it—two people who have never really lived together at all, suddenly undertake to do just that in a pledged devotion to each other for the rest of their lives! Each one leaves his precious independence at the altar, and come what may, for better or for worse, restricts his and her earthly destinies to the care and keeping of the other.

This joining together of destinies has a frightening quality about it. The good fortune of one will be the good fortune of the other, and sorrow or loss for one will be sorrow or loss for the other. Failure and disgrace will be shared, sickness as well as health. Blessings will often have to make way for burdens in this shared life. The very achievement of personal intimacy will in turn create seemingly insuperable problems, leading inevitably to some severe crises. Each partner shall render the other vulnerable to a high degree because of the intimate knowledge that rises out of close sharing. Yet, withal, marriage cannot be less than a total commitment, and such commitments must be accepted on the basis of the realization that each life will be laid open to a new range of hurts and burdens not possible previously. As each one shares in all that touches the other, life takes on a double risk and responsibility.

In the non-Christian approach to marriage the commitments can be conditional; to many couples they do not represent finality. In the Christian approach this cannot be. Christian marriage is a radical thing when gauged by secular standards; it makes radical demands and offers radical rewards. It points to a radically different center around which all is to find cohesion and unity. This unifying center is the Person of Christ! In Christian thinking it takes three to make a marriage; Christ makes Christian marriage a three-dimensional affair.

The great question at the heart of all human relations, not the least of which is marriage, is: What purpose is at the heart of this relation that is not ultimately selfish? Only the Christian concept proposes for marriage a purpose that is not selfish. This purpose is plainly set forth in the Scriptures. It is not little short of tragedy that the average professing Christian is seldom instructed and so is unable intelligently to outline the divine purpose of the marital union?

Except for several qualifying statements of the Apostle Paul which are directed toward unique situations, the Scriptures teach consistently that marriage is God's norm for nearly every person. That God sometimes appoints an individual to a life of single status is the rare exception, and then evidently it is that one may conform to a special call of God for service where such a status is best suited to its fulfillment. Marriage is the norm nonetheless, as is readily seen in the fact that there are basic personality needs the fulfillment of which is possible to the highest degree only in the experience of marriage oneness. The achievement of personal intimacy at the deepest levels, for one thing, or mutual responsibility and concern in love—these are fulfillments best afforded in marriage. Yet there must be no doubt that whenever God should clearly appoint an individual to single status in order to carry out a particu-

lar calling, those personal fulfillments which are thereby
rendered impossible shall not necessarily warp the personality or restrict the life. It is obvious that this might
happen and does happen, but it need not. The Lord
Jesus Christ is perfectly able to compensate these deficiencies in other ways. His compensations always transcend the losses in life which are suffered for His sake,
and this is no less true in the lives of the unmarried.
There are far greater sorrows in life than that of remaining single. The rule for young people, however,
should be to live by the principle that unless God definitely directs otherwise for a known purpose relating to
His service, one should expect and plan for marriage,
and should pray for the guidance of God in this matter.
One effect of thus planning on marriage will be the adjustment to normal social activities where one would be
most likely to meet the person of God's choice. This
whole matter of how to find the right person will concern us extensively in a later chapter.

Unfortunately for our age of quick-service-counter
answers to nearly all questions, there are no neat little
formulas for determining when one is in love. Nor is it a
simple process of discovering the person of God's
choice as a life partner. Infatuation is a powerful force
in human relations because of the constant operation of
certain principles of attraction between the sexes. The
distinction between love and infatuation must be made
by young people at a time in their maturation when they
are neither experienced in making such decisions nor
emotionally able to do so with any great degree of assurance. Cultural emphases are potent, and emotional
demands can quite readily assume the mastery over rational approaches to love and marriage. Nor is infatuation a problem for adolescent and unmarried persons
only; it can invade the sacred precincts of the finest and

happiest marriage, and will sometimes do so during the best and latest years.

The Christian concept alters many aspects of courtship and marriage. For one thing, superior to the statement, "She seems *made* for me," is the alternate "She seems *meant for me.*" The first might be said with some degree of reality in any one of a number of possibilities. The second will better express the Christian conviction that one has found God's will.

The expression "made for me" assumes evidence of compatibility, which evidence is generally superficial and external. It may simply stand for: "I love me and want you, because you make me happy." This is at the very core of infatuation as we shall see. It is no more an adequate criterion than that of the young fellow who says: "I know I am in love because she makes me feel so good when we are together." The good feeling may arise from one of a number of causes beside love.

Marriage is not meant to be the pairing off of two selfish individuals for the purpose of mutual exploitation. Pooled selfishness may lead to the enjoyment of each other, but never to the true identification of two persons in responsible marriage. Our chief concern in these pages will be to determine how one can be sure that the choice of a marriage partner can be made on grounds other than those of mutual attraction to external qualities, or presumably perfect compatibility as suggested by infatuation. The Christian wants to know the purpose of God in marriage as such, and then specifically what the will of God is for him personally in the choice of a life mate.

The gospel of Christian marriage (for surely it is the "good news" of marriage success) proclaims that Christ is adequate to every problem that might emerge from the marriage relation. Particularly is He adequate to that central difficulty, the innate selfishness of sinful persons. Is not self-devotion, as Shelley called it "the dark idolatry of self," the chief problem of everyone? Is it not prevalent among Christian people perhaps only a little less than among those who do not profess to know Christ? Is it not selfish pride that precipitates most marital crises?

The problem of self-devotion is accentuated in marriage, because there is where personal intimacy reaches its highest achievement. Two self-centered lives confront each other in the most self-revealing terms. Each challenges the freedom and self-love of the other as they have never been challenged before. In marriage self-love is crucial, for it is the very antithesis of the kind of love that gives cohesion to the shared life. Marriage amounts to the exposé of the independently-minded, self-directed and self-devoted person. Nothing essential in personality development is altered simply because one takes a marriage vow. Before the high and holy ideals of Christian love and oneness, the love and wisdom of the individual are found wanting. The only solution is Christ preeminent in the life. Each one before His sovereign Lordship must consent to the destruction of proud ego as a necessary condition for the fulfillment of their married oneness. When the love and power of the indwelling Christ are allowed to transcend the inadequacies of human marriage, they will also transform marriage to make it conform to the divine pattern.

The most advanced ideal of marriage in its non-Christian form is expressed by the word "togetherness." The same ideal in its Christian form is expressed by the word "oneness." As the highest aspects of personal life are spiritual, so the highest aspects of marriage are likewise spiritual. No individual is an end in himself, and neither is marriage an end in itself. Marriage is a means to an end. The great trouble is that, for the non-Christian, marriage is the means to selfish personal ends. To the Christian, marriage is the means to the fulfillment of divine ends. The marriage union, like man himself, is designed for the glory of God, and for the exhibition of His purposes of love on earth.

At the same time, marriage is the fulfillment of two lives in mutuality, and it is a union created as a means of fulfilling a larger purpose of God through those two lives made one. Personal fulfillment, as high an ideal as it is, must not obscure the fact that it is not the only purpose in marriage. Out of this human relation must also emerge a divine dimension, the fulfillment of a spiritual purpose outside of the two persons. So the Christian couple dedicate themselves, not only each to the other, but both to God. Oneness in Christ, and oneness in their service for Christ, complete the purpose of marriage.

Christ calls the church His "bride," pointing to the marriage relationship as the most perfect symbol of that between Himself and believers. This oneness was made possible by the Saviour's suffering love and costly death. It is a relationship established upon the fact of His resurrection and ascension. The living Christ incorporates the trusting individual into a vital relationship with Himself. The two figures employed by the Apostle to express this union speak of the Christian as a member of the Body of Christ, and as the Bride of Christ. The Christian is made an actual partaker of Christ, sharing His very life through the Holy Spirit. As glorious as the fact of reconciliation may be, more glorious is the fact of actual union and communion! Personal intimacy with Christ is one of the distinctive features of the Christian revelation. What possibilities of personal fulfillment and intimacy are suggested by this spiritual relation! What privileges inhere in creative Christian oneness in marriage!

Since Christian marriage oneness has Christ as the

dynamic and unifying center, it is not difficult to see why Scripture admonishes strongly: "Be not unequally yoked together with unbelievers." A believer and an unbeliever could never achieve oneness in marriage, only togetherness. Their marriage might appear very successful and as having a high degree of personal happiness, but it would never reach the potentialities of fulfillment that would be possible if God's blessing were upon it, and it fulfilled the purposes of God. As it has been quaintly put: "For a child of God to marry a child of the Devil is to have Satan for his father-in-law!" What a complication of the in-law problem that is!

The real as well as symbolic oneness of the marriage relation was purposed for man from the very beginning. It was within the realm of perfect realization for our first parents. Such personal intimacy as they originally enjoyed with God was theirs to enjoy with each other. In the beginning there was one will, God's will. But sin introduced another will into the universe that God had willed into being. That sinful will destroyed the basis of union and the unbroken experience of intimacy between man and his Creator-Sovereign. The direct consequence was the cessation of full personal intimacy between the man and his wife. The will that separates man from God is the will that separates man from his wife. The objective reality of union which marriage was to symbolize was shattered, the divine purpose in marriage obscured, and its fulfillment rendered impossible.

The very origin of human sinfulness reveals what is at the heart of man's disorder. The woman took the prerogative of directing the husband, and the husband took the prerogative of heeding. The woman exerted a will other than God's will in directing her husband, and the man exerted a will other than God's in heeding her. There was no longer a single will on earth, God's will!

God's perfect order has been replaced by man's disorder! It is the problem of many wills.

Monogamous and indissoluble marriage continues as the design of God, but it is an area where human sinfulness persistently manifests itself. Human love at best is inherently tragic, marred by human selfishness and sinfulness. The sinful and self-centered life cannot fulfill the requisites of love as demanded by a successful marriage. Human marriage at its highest must experience conflict and pain.

Since human sinfulness is deeply involved in the problem of marriage, it is well that we have a working definition. Sinfulness is essentially the improper relatedness of man with God, man with man, and man with himself, as a consequence of his wilful independence of God. Rejecting God as his sovereign, man became his own god, his own sovereign. ("Why just be *like* God? Why not *be* God?") Choosing no longer to have God as the center of his life, man was left a single alternative: he must have himself as the center of his life. He himself is the end for which he lives. As the rightful Sovereign is no longer the object of all man's living, man himself must be that object. Such a self-centered, self-motivated life can never fulfill the requisites of love demanded in marriage.

We have already noted that marriage was instituted not only as an earthly symbol of the spiritual relation between God and man, but it was given for man's sake too. It was God's provision for a need within man, the creature. Man needed union and communion with another equally a person like himself, who had needs like his own. But while the woman is sufficiently like man in his essential nature as to share a mutal understanding and common life, she is of a complementary nature. The needs and capabilities of each one differ in such a way as to make it possible for each to fulfill the needs of the other. Their very differences form the basis for mutual attraction, each finding in the other that which would fulfill what was lacking in his own nature. This mutual longing for the other was to bring an experience of fulfillment to both, and the quality that was to transcend all others in bringing this about was to be love. In loving, each would experience an outgoingness, a caring for another that would not be content with less than a personal commitment. This union of two persons as husband and wife would mean more to them both than their individual lives alone could ever mean to them separately. And in such an intimate union, each partner will come to understand something unique about his own nature and the nature of the other.

Personal intimacy can be achieved at every level of being: spiritual, rational, social, emotional, and physical. Such intimacy in a permanent commitment of two persons is meant to be the experience of every Christian husband and wife. Through the redemption that is in Christ, man can first be restored to the place of personal union and communion with God. With a new sense of belonging, and a new experience of the love of God, a person is set free to love once again. Whenever this personal experience is shared by both a husband and a wife, they have a redeemed marriage. The same redeeming love and the same experience of forgiveness and dependence upon God will permeate the whole marriage relationship with spiritually transforming power.

A Christian marriage can never fail, but the people in that marriage can fail. There is a vast difference between the two possibilities. So if the marriage of two Christians seems to fail, it is either that they were ignorant of God's purpose, or unwilling to commit themselves to it.

The Christian concept as we have formulated it thus

far is expressed concisely in the word "oneness." The highest non-Christian concept is expressed in the word "togetherness." This idea of togetherness may mean no more than what is expressed in the superficial notion that another person "is made for me." The idea of oneness may mean the conviction that the other person "is meant for me" as the gift of God's will. The concept of oneness, on the contrary, implies the fusing of two lives into one life in a growing experience of true mutuality.

Now that two persons are both related to the Lord Jesus Christ and to each other in marriage, they have Him as the unifying center of their shared life. This center is outside of themselves, transcending their individual wills with His will, their strength with His strength, and their love with His love. Just as completely as they are individually united with Him will they be united with one another. This is the high and holy goal set before Christian couples.

Fundamentally, Christian marriage is more than finding the right person; it is being the right person. To be that right person one must be rightly related to Christ not only as Saviour, but also as Lord. To have His Lordship means that one must bring one's old self-life to terms at His cross. It means experiencing the forgiving grace and love of Christ in daily life. The old independent and self-willed life must be crucified with Christ, and a new life in Him taken up.

The individual Christian believer enters into oneness with Christ as Lord of the daily life when he can say with Paul, "I am crucified with Christ: nevertheless I live; yet not I, but Christ liveth in me: and the life which I now live in the flesh I live by the faith of the Son of God, who loved me, and gave himself for me" (Galatians 2:20). That this is a very personal thing is indicated by the eight personal pronouns. Translate this with a change in pronoun and it stands for the way in which the Christian couple comes into oneness with Christ in the daily life: "We are crucified with Christ, nevertheless we live; yet not we, but Christ liveth in us: and the life which we now live in the flesh we live by the faith of the Son of God, who loved us, and gave himself for us." This is one relation of surrender in which it is possible to say "we" without any loss of individuality whatsoever! This is true oneness as Christ would establish it.

There is a popular concept often expressed in this way: "Marriage is a fifty-fifty affair. He gives up 50 per cent of his way, and she gives up 50 per cent of her way, so they will have a perfect 100 per cent happiness." But marriage is far more than a give and take. In this concept it is the remaining 50 per cent of "his way" plus the 50 per cent of "her way" that will add up to a perfect 100 per cent—of trouble!

For the Christian couple, marriage should be "one new life existent in two persons." Here is equal dignity and worth, and the recognition of the individual place of each; here is true oneness at every level of being and doing. As Elton Trueblood has suggested, a successful marriage is not one in which two people, beautifully matched, find each other and get along happily ever after because of this initial matching. It is, instead, a system by means of which persons who are sinful and contentious are so caught up by a dream and a purpose bigger than themselves that they work through the years, in spite of repeated disappointment, to make the dream come true.

The secret is wilful surrender of self and selves to Christ. While it would be degrading for one ego to give up to another ego, it is a blessed and exalting thing for both together to surrender up their wills to Him. He consents to give up all of his independent will and desire, and she consents to give up all of her independent will and desire, and together they seek the will of God in all things. This is far more than each one merely turning from self to live for the other, as selfless as that might seem to be; it is rather both living together for Him. Each for the other, and both for Christ—this is the two-way direction of outgoing love in Christian marriage.

The Costly Option of Lonely Individualism

Scripture relates the creation of woman as taking place in the context of a striking circumstance in the economy of God. Man had been created as a personal being who reflected the very image of God, dependent upon his Creator in every way, yet experiencing the personal intimacy of unhindered communion with God. Man was not complete in himself, but had need of such intimacy with God. Man's nature had an appointed deficit that could only be filled by means of union and communion with God.

But man was given an appointed deficit that made him dependent in still another way. Just as he could complete himself spiritually only as he lived in personal interaction with God, so likewise he could complete himself and reach adulthood only as he lived in interaction with other human persons. This interaction of personalities is the necessary condition for the maturing and fulfilling of personality. The appointed deficit in man was really the provision of a majestic potential.

We have already seen that it is not merely a society of men that is needed. God made the woman with a complementary nature that there might be a basis for attraction and mutual fulfillment. An individual man is attracted to an individual woman, and each finds the possibility of fulfilling the life of the other. Each has the capacity to complete the other; they complement in order to complete each other.

In Genesis 2:18 we read: "It is not good that man should be alone. . . ." Who said that? God Himself said that. Did He suddenly observe an imperfection in an otherwise perfect design? No, indeed! God is simply pointing out to us that He appointed this deficit in man by himself, in order that we might perceive the design of God in providing the woman to be man's wife.

Milton observed in one of his tracts: "Loneliness is the first thing which God's eye named not good." The alternative to personal fulfillment through the shared life is social isolation and an accompanying sense of loneliness. This form of individualism is a costly and desolating thing.

Marriage is the most perfect relation in which personal intimacy can be achieved. But even the marriage relation can be invaded by individualism and emptied of its meaning and purpose, with the result so that there can be little more than a mutual loneliness. Our next chapter will deal with the whole question of the crucial need for personal intimacy in marriage, its hazards and hopes. In preparation for this, let us trace the working of personal isolation, noting the high cost that loneliness exacts in human life.

Loneliness arises not from isolation in space, but from isolation in spirit. It is not a geographical problem, but a social problem. It concerns man's relatedness to others beside himself. Personal isolation is the cause of loneliness, and as Alexander Magoun points out, that loneliness becomes an emotional sickness which feeds upon itself. As love is outgoing, loneliness is ingrowing. The lonely individual may feel as though he were willing to sell his soul to be loved and thus to identify himself satisfyingly with another person.

Loneliness on the human plane results in part from

the illusion sinful man indulges that he can live with other persons without committing himself to share in their concerns, or entering into a responsible interdependence. Probably the loneliest person in the world, as Roy Burkhart observes, is the one who apparently has everything except a reverence for other personalities, and so does not know what it is to be committed to the needs of others, or creatively to fulfill his life through interaction. The walls between persons which are created by our culture can only be scaled by the kind of concerned love that does care and share. The deepest needs in human life are met by love and acceptance. The reaction which arises when these needs are not met manifests itself in the form of a frustrating loneliness, and there is certainly no more frustrating experience in life than that of loneliness! The destructive power of long-term loneliness is frightful! The love and acceptance which come from personal sharing are experiences without which the burden of being human becomes intolerable.

Rollo May has suggested that the basic problem of loneliness is enhanced by the fact that we are isolated, alienated individuals, produced in a society in which competitive individualism has been the dominant goal. We are, indeed, what T. S. Eliot called "the hollow men." How much of life shows itself to be man's desperate attempt to secure himself against the void within, to buoy himself up against even the conscious awareness of that void! But though one may keep "dated up" in the attempt to hold his loneliness at bay, a crisis must come sooner or later. Even excessive dedication to material or social pursuits will not alleviate the condition or hold off the crisis for long.

Personal isolation and its resultant loneliness are contradictions of the very ends for which we were made. Any form of personal detachment which inhibits personal intimacy with others is an affront to the worth and potential of human personality as God ordered it. No wonder loneliness generates its own dreadful brand of anxiety and fear, frustration and resentment, and eventually even hostility and hate! The lonely self will react violently in an attempt sooner or later to break out of the isolation that has caused so much pain.

Karen Horney says that neurosis is "a disturbance in one's relation to self and others." Imagine, then, the neurotic loneliness that is precipitated by the feeling of unrelatedness toward God and toward others, and especially toward one's husband or wife! Here is the crux of an enormous problem at the heart of the two highest relationships of life, one's relatedness to God and to one's wife or husband.

Loneliness, then, tells us two things of great importance about ourselves. First, it reflects the fact that each person knows that no other human person can perfectly share the secret of the inner self. God alone can perfectly enter into our deepest thoughts and feelings. Each person's life is ultimately bound up to God alone, whether one would have it that way or not. Only God can know the fears and anxieties that dwell in the inner citadel of the soul. Only He can know the longing after goodness and the heartbreak over sinful failure. Only He can know the true hopes and ambitions which motivate one's life. Only He can know the compulsions which control an individual person. Yes, one's real life is shut up to God alone, whether one chooses it that way or not.

The second thing that loneliness tells us about ourselves is that we were designed for community with other persons. Humanity is possible only as community; this is a basic principle of great significance. Only through interaction with others can we fulfill ourselves. Insofar as loneliness tells us the truth about ourselves, as James Pike reminds us, and insofar as loneliness leads us to establish these relationships, it is a good thing. Loneliness is really more than one of the occupational hazards of being human; it is the voice of God calling us back to the truth of our lives as they were meant to be. This truth of personal intimacy as the true antidote to loneliness is to occupy our attention more fully in the pages that follow.

The tender care of God acts to bring us reconciliation with Himself and thus into relatedness with Him once again. In relatedness with Him we have the scales removed from our eyes to see the possibility of relatedness with other persons through the same experience of love and concern. We see clearly that human unrelatedness, with its painful loneliness and frustration, roots deeper in the fact of unrelatedness to God. It is this unrelatedness to God that causes man his fundamental restlessness and frustration in the total picture of his life. But man can leave his self-exile from God when he chooses to return to Him through the redemption of Christ. No longer need he endure creature-loneliness as one detached from his rightful Sovereign.

The tragedy of many lies in their attempt to substitute some human relatedness for relatedness to God through Christ. This is understandable insofar as many are ignorant of the possibilities in redemption. Nonetheless, it is cause for sorrow that so many are attempting to satisfy their longing by seeking to achieve personal intimacy with others equally lonely and detached, and whose fundamental need for relatedness to God is just as great. Doubtless this is true in many marriages, for countless persons expect a marriage partner to fill the vacancy within themselves that only God can fill.

The Genesis record tells us that the loneliness of an unmarried person is thus more than a psychological feeling; it is the condition of being less than a complete person. God's design as we have seen is to secure a real completeness between a husband and wife. This is beautifully set forth in the opening pages of our Bible.

God said: "I will make a help meet for him." We commonly use the word "helpmate" as a single word; the Hebrew original has two words: "helper meet" for him. The lexicons tell us that woman was given to be a "complement, counterpart, one suitable to" him. Or as one puts it: "one who answers back to him" (not suggesting her ability to retort, I'm sure!). She answers to his needs and fulfills his potentials. As another puts it: "one who fills up his empty places" (which doesn't necessarily mean "All I do is cook for that man!"). The woman fills up the man's essential needs and completes his selfhood.

The "helper meet for him" is more than someone to divide the labor of his life. She is someone to share his life, to draw man out of himself and into a wider of circle of life that involves completion through interaction with another. Each partner in the marriage assists the other to complete himself.

Genesis 2:22-24 reads: "And the rib, which the Lord God had taken from man, made He woman, and brought her unto the man. And Adam said, This is now bone of my bones, and flesh of my flesh: she shall be called Woman, because she was taken out of Man. Therefore shall a man leave his father and his mother, and shall cleave unto his wife: and they shall be one flesh." This term "one flesh" speaks of the unique oneness which God intends. It is a total commitment to intimacy in all of life together, symbolized by the sexual union of one flesh.

To "cleave unto his wife" means making one out of two. It was Harry Rimmer who pointed out that this is just the opposite of what the butcher means when he uses the word "cleave" when he makes two out of one!

Perhaps modern marriage has mistaken the use of the word!

So God took a "rib" from man to make the woman. My friend, Carl Thomas, recalls writing to Helen during the war, before she became Mrs. Thomas, addressing her "My dear floating rib." But whatever the proud male may choose to think, the fact that God took woman from the side of man does not make her a side issue! Or as the student wrote in his essay: "After man came woman and she has been after him ever since."

All humor aside, there is a beautiful and profound suggestion in this. A Rabbinical comment puts it this way: "The man is restless while he misses the rib that was taken out of his side, and the woman is restless until she gets under the man's arm from whence she was taken." Here is really a majestic statement of the equality and mutuality that elevates women to the place they enjoy in Christian thought.

For both husband and wife this truth leads to glory and to humility. It is humbling to the woman to know that she was created for the man, but it is to her glory to know that she alone can complete him. Likewise, it is humbling to the man to know that he is incomplete without the woman, but it is to his glory to know that the woman was created for him!

We pause here merely to take note of something that shall receive considerable attention farther on. The sexual function is not simply a means of procreation; it symbolizes and objectifies the unique oneness of the married couple. It is a hallowed declaration more eloquent than words of the miracle of marriage oneness. It speaks of more than physical completion, and represents the mystery of oneness being achieved by two individual persons. And this design for personal completion is the very reason why marriage is intended to be monogamous and indissoluble. The sexual union must be uniquely just a part of life between the husband and the wife for it must speak of the fact that together they make one whole. That whole, once established, is not to be divided again. Marital infidelity is a denial of oneness, a rejection of God's design. And since it substitutes man's disorder for God's order, no real happiness can ever emerge from it, nor any real satisfaction of any kind. It can never lead to fulfillment of any kind either. It is for the reason of completion and oneness that sexuality without mutuality is a fraud, an empty experience that fails to communicate the values for which it was given. For either it must express oneness, the intimacy of all of life together and the mutual concern of two persons who love and care for each other, or it is a hollow act without substantial meaning. God knew what He was doing when He put the lock in wedlock!

The husband according to his function becomes a lover, a provider, a protector, a family head, and the wife becomes the beloved, the companion, the homemaker, the child-bearer. Each becomes distinctly much more besides. And yet each one is just one-half of the new creation; the union is everything! Creative oneness is paramount!

Oneness in Christ is the great essential, the very hub of the wheel of married life. Where such spiritual oneness exists there will be an atmosphere in which oneness will most likely be achieved at every other level of life together.

So the wife is the true counterpart and complement to the husband. Life and love are reciprocal in an equality of dignity and worth. Each is necessary to the other, and though the functions are not the same, they are of equal importance. A woman is not man's property, but his partner!

There is then a mutual dignity by virtue of the fact that each is necessary for the completion of the other. It is the perversion of this principle that rightly seems grotesque, when a man tries to imitate a woman and gives up his masculinity, or a woman tries to imitate a man and gives up her femininity. Only when the man and the woman fulfill their rightful place is there beauty and order and creativeness after the divine pattern.

The equality that makes possible a mutuality and oneness between two persons, who are committed to each other in marriage, has been beautifully set forth by another:

If God meant woman to rule over man, He would have taken her out of Adam's head. Had He designed her to be his slave, He would have taken her out of his feet. But God took woman out of man's side, for He made her to be a helpmate and an equal to him.

—Augustine

The Scripture consistently teaches the equalitarian and democratic nature of marriage. There cannot be true oneness except as there is equal dignity and status. The wife who came from man's side is to stand at his side to share every responsibility, and to enjoy every privilege.

2. QUEST FOR PERSONAL INTIMACY

How subtle and deep are the basic needs of personal life! Not the least of these is the need for achieving a satisfying experience of personal intimacy. The human relation where God intends that this might be most perfectly achieved is marriage. If marriage is a living symbol of the oneness between the Christian and his Lord, then the possibility of personal intimacy becomes exciting indeed. In this possibility of complete and satisfying personal intimacy, Christian marriage takes on and exhibits a glorious uniqueness. It is precisely in this that Christian marriage is set off from all lesser concepts of the marriage union, a lofty ideal yet at the same time a most practical relationship.

Commonly, when speaking of marriage, the term "intimacy" is used in reference to sexual intimacy exclusively. Our day has strangely majored on a minor in the matter of sexual intimacy. This is only one of many areas of married life where intimacy can be experienced, so that consistently to restrict the meaning of the word to sexual intimacy is to expose a deficiency in the popular concept of what marriage really is.

All too often the romantic illusion that intimacy is created and sustained by the sexual union obscures the higher possibility of achieving intimacy throughout the whole range of the personal relationship in marriage. We are concerned in this chapter to explore this higher possibility. The role of sexual intimacy is not to be minimized, of course, but this is hardly the danger in our culture. We shall here examine the fuller personal intimacy of which sexual intimacy is a vital but a subordinate part.

This fascinating possibility takes us deep into the territory of life-sharing. We see human relations at their deepest levels. This is hallowed ground! The mystery at the very heart of Christian marriage is a divine mystery. Personal intimacy in marriage is a costly thing, and we shall not penetrate the nature of it without seeing something of the costliness of God's love for us, and the relation between human intimacy and the intimacy of man with God which was made possible by the sacrifice of Christ. The two cannot be separated. Human love is inherently tragic because of sinfulness, so that human love must be redeemed if it is to function as love at all. Successful married love is not forged without tension and conflict that may at times threaten the very continuance of the marriage. Love adequate to manage conflict is not indigenous to human nature, nor is it easily come by. So our examination must bring into perspective all that personal intimacy in marriage means, face realistically its costs, and evaluate its alternatives.

To begin with, we need a working definition of this quality we call personal intimacy: "Personal intimacy in marriage is a relation in which husband and wife grow in their knowledge and understanding of each other, so as to share their lives completely in a common identification of purpose, and support each other in a mutual commitment of love, trust, and fidelity."

A distinctively Christian marriage takes place whenever a husband and wife covenant a permanent relation of personal intimacy as defined above, at the same time making this relation subservient to their commitment to Christ. The highest purpose uniting them is their acceptance of the will of God for every area of their life together, and in their love for Him they find their own. Their marriage then becomes a spiritual covenant of mutual love and trust through the sharing of life together. This is more than a contract, for a contract is a mere lifeless, legal thing, whereas a covenant is a living, personal, and sacred pledge between two persons, supported by mutual love and respect, trust and fidelity.

The Measure of Marriage Success

It is not too much to say that the success or failure of any marriage may be measured in terms of the personal intimacy achieved. Since true intimacy can only be achieved in a commitment of mutual love and trust, the necessary components of every marriage, this establishes a basic test of marriage adjustment and success. There must be mutuality in marriage, the possibility of a reciprocal action of love and "secret sympathy" between husband and wife. Such mutuality requires the full acceptance in equal respect and trust of each partner by the other. Without question, the highest degree of mutuality is established whenever the one regards the other as created in God's image, infinitely precious in His sight, the object of redeeming grace and love. It is upon this foundation of mutual love, respect, and concern that personal intimacy can be forged within Christian marriage.

The value and danger of personal intimacy in marriage may seem generally quite obvious. Closer analysis, we believe, will disclose a greater tension between its hopes and hazards than is usually conceived.

To grasp the idea of man's capacity for such intimacy we must go over some of the same ground touched upon in the last chapter, but more thoroughly, in order to establish a correlation between marriage intimacy and the higher spiritual intimacy of man's relation to

God. We must be persuaded, before we can go very far, that man's need for personal intimacy is rooted in the very nature of his relation to God. For if this is undeniably true, then we can proceed to an understanding of why man craves such intimacy on the human level, and seeks it especially within marriage.

Design for Intimacy

The Scriptures plainly teach that God designed man with the capacity for personal intimacy. In fact, God created man for the first purpose of establishing an intimate relation between man and Himself. While we cannot say that this originated from a need in the economy of God, we can affirm at least, as Scripture does, that this was a desire upon God's part, something He Himself sovereignly willed to bring about. This fact is implicit in God's declaration that He created man "in his own image." This speaks worlds to us both about God and about man. Whatever else is meant by "the image of God," it is plain that man has been given a personality likeness to God, a capacity for consciously sharing a common life with the Almighty through communion and fellowship of a personal nature.

Five observable features of human personality exhibit on what gound this intimate fellowship between God and man is possible. We will trace them briefly.

(1) *Intelligence* is a personal capacity that shows man's endowment from God. Man is a rational being, and as such he has the capacity for knowing and understanding God, His nature, acts, and will. It is possible, by means of intelligent interaction, for God and man to enter understandingly into the very being of one another. *Personal intimacy is a rational relationship.*

(2) *Emotional feeling* is a capacity which reflects the image of God in human personality. All of man's

knowledge and experience has this effect upon him, that he reacts feelingly to the facts and relations of life. He has attitudes of love and hate, of sympathy and hostility, of concern and indifference, etc. Personal intimacy is fulfilled especially as two persons reciprocate such feelings as love and sympathy. Out of such emotions come human tenderness and kindness, as well as responsible concern for other persons. Is it not an incredible fact that God made His human creatures to receive love and to reciprocate it, and thus to enter into the very purposes of God with sympathetic concern? *Personal intimacy is an emotionally felt relationship.*

(3) *Freedom of will,* the capacity for making personal choices, is an attribute of God's personality now imaged in man. There could have been no such thing as human responsibility were it not for the freedom to make personal responses which God gave to man. What value would attach to personal intimacy between man and God were it not for the capacity of free and spontaneous response of free volition on man's part? *Personal intimacy is a freely willed relationship.*

(4) *Moral judgment* is a mysterious quality of human personality as designed and given by God. Man has a vivid sense of the moral quality of all his free acts. There is in every person a sense of "ought" and "ought not." Whatever one's particular moral standard, men everywhere are morally motivated. They invariably express themselves by using such words of moral import as "right . . . wrong, good . . . bad," etc.

There is in every person an inner monitor called conscience. After dropping out of psychological literature for awhile, the term is back once again. Moral responsibility is universally regarded as a fundamental capacity of human personality. Personal intimacy is possible because of the existence of such moral qualities as trust, fidelity, etc. *Personal intimacy is a moral relationship.*

(5) *Spiritual awareness* is a capacity of human personality. Man derives his sense of ultimate worth and dignity from his sense of relation to God. He longs for the completion of his own personality through interaction with a perfect personality with whom he can sustain an abiding relation. This perfect personality he intuitively associates with his Creator and Sovereign. Man will not settle for dust and drudgery as the be-all and end-all of life, but would discover his own true self in relation to Deity. *Personal intimacy is a spiritual relationship.*

Intimacy Lost and Restored

The sum of our present thoughts is that man was originally furnished for a most wonderful intimacy with God. But we have already briefly considered how what God designed and brought into being, sin marred and perverted. All five capacities of human personality were so altered as to be reduced to utter inability so far as any adequate relatedness to God was concerned. Man could no longer know and understand God in rational intimacy. Man could no longer receive and reciprocate divine love in emotional intimacy with God. Man could no longer freely will the blessed relationship of personal intimacy with God. Man could no longer direct his motives by the divine "ought." And man could no longer appraise human life as having worth and dignity through relatedness to God.

Every attribute of human personality was perverted from its original intent, no longer imaging God. In choosing separation from God, man elected to violate the very purpose for which he was made. What remained was an aching void within, a sense of his isolation from all that God must be, and a loneliness he could not quite understand.

The human creature, wherever he is found, suffers deeply and profoundly as a result of this loss of personal intimacy with God. In his longing for a relatedness that satisfies his need, he continuously seeks intimacy with other humankind, only to be frustrated on every hand. No other human person can fully enter into the inner secret of one's personal life.

Such human restlessness ceases only when a redemptive relation is established between man the rebel and God the Saviour. Coming to Christ, the trusting sinner finds satisfying reconciliation with God, and that paves the way for restored intimacy with God. The fundamental relatedness of life is once again repaired. Reconciliation and intimacy are experienced upon the ground of God's redeeming grace and love. Not the least of the wonders to which the trusting sinner is introduced is the knowledge that God's purpose and desire to draw man back into personal intimacy with Himself cost God everything! It cost forgiving love, suffering love! It cost God His own Son. And this cost God assumed despite all human unworthiness. God's transcendent love, outgoing toward sinful man, makes personal intimacy with Him such a priceless privilege! Imagine! Fully known yet fully loved; what glorious intimacy is this!

For the Christian, marriage is intended to be a secondary fulfillment of this very experience at the level of two human persons, husband and wife. For the non-Christian, marriage is an attempted solution to the need for intimacy, but apart from God's love and grace. This attempt is doomed to certain disappointment. For the Christian couple there is the possibility of attaining a high degree of intimacy, enriched by the sense of their relation to Christ, an intimacy on earth that reflects the intimacy that reaches into heaven.

Modern Society Complicates the Problem

Nearly everything in modern life is aligned against much experience of personal intimacy outside of the home. Marriage is a social institution and as such it is affected by the changing social order. It has been enormously influenced by the following three social forces that have gained momentous power in the past fifty years or so.

First, *industrialization* is a social force operating against personal intimacy. An industrial society has brought with it the mass man. More often than not today, a man finds himself an impersonal cog in a giant machine. His competitive relation to other individuals drives him along with but a single remaining motive, to be a success at any price. He lives in a culture that places more importance upon being a success in business than upon being a success as a man.

In business and industry men must try to get along with as little personal conflict as possible, for they are not regarded as persons but as performers. A man must reveal as little as possible his individual differences of opinion, habit, or taste. He is accepted so long as he proves himself acceptable; he is not accepted for himself. Hence he learns to hide this true feelings, to disguise his fears and inadequacies behind a façade of superiority, and to affect a cold efficiency in all things. Any personal intimacy with others in his workaday world might disclose his weaknesses, create distrust on the part of associates, and possibly precipitate loss of prestige. Personal intimacy has become a dangerous thing inasmuch as it might threaten his very security in life. No pleasure arising out of such intimacy in the present must be permitted to jeopardize one's chances for the future. Industrialization and the mechanized age have imposed an impersonal condition upon the masses of men, to block the fulfillment of a personal need. Men by the thousand commute to work in their own automobiles alone rather than socialize with others on public transportation. Those who do elect to use public transportation secure themselves behind the newspaper as a haven against any concern that might be shown for them or that they might feel responsible to show to others.

Secondly, *urbanization* is a social force operating directly against personal intimacy. People more and more are being collected together in the great population centers, the modern cities. Man's biggest claim today is anonymity. Very few men work in the same place as their neighbor. Their workday is separated from both home and neighborhood. A man can have one set of friends and associates at work, another at home and in the neighborhood, and the two may never meet. In fact, a man scarcely knows his neighbors for he neither works with them nor lives socially with them. Their only thing in common is residence in the same neighborhood.

Thirdly, *mobility* is a social force operating against personal intimacy. Countless men and women live in mobile communities where they have few, if any, personal roots. Whether a family moves from the community or stays put, their community is affected by constant change. Its identity does not long remain the same. Spreading urban life introduces cycles of change into the character of the community, disrupting its identity.

If a family chooses to move out farther, say into the suburbs, it means establishing new roots. This does not greatly affect the husband who spends his day somewhere else anyway, but it affects the wife and children. But if the family stays in the old community in order to preserve its roots, friends move from around them and strangers move in. Their community life suffers change in either case.

But mobility has another dimension; individuals are on the move socially. The automobile and superhighway have radically changed the social habits of men and women. It is not only that men commute farther to work, but social activity is no longer restricted to the community where a family lives. People have even become so selective in the matter of churches as to think nothing of traveling some distance to the church of their choice, despite the fact that that church has no relation to life in their community.

The effect of this mobility is that personal intimacy has become highly restricted in modern life. All the more do husbands and wives seek such intimacy primarily in their marriage relation. It is important to note what added demands these social fractures have placed upon modern marriage.

How different the life of yesteryear, the life of the small communities, where everyone knew everyone else and community life was largely that of personal interdependence. Each person accepted the other for what that other was in himself, and as part of the community. Success did not depend so much upon one's superior performance, or upon the affectation of superior qualities. Social aloofness was unthought of except perhaps in the upper classes. Lives were more transparent and open. The personal quality was more important than impersonal achievement, a person could afford to be himself in his community relations. People learned to manage their differences and to share their struggles and tragedies.

In those days men and women achieved independence by marrying and leaving the paternal home. The necessary functions of their newly formed family life tended to give cohesion to their marriage. They shared many domestic tasks now taken over by laborsaving devices in the home or agencies outside the home. Family members were economically dependent then.

Fifty years ago, social life centered in the home, and people were participants rather than spectators in the realm of entertainment. Families did things together as a unit, whereas modern society has made recreational specialists out of family members, with a multiplicity of organizations clamoring for the separate interests of family members. Whether we want it or not, the family of today is separating by centrifugal force. Home is no longer self-sufficient economically or socially. There are not even the pressures of the community to keep marriages together as there once were. As W. T. Thompson reminds us, home may be facetiously referred to as "the place where we put the things we buy."

Even conflict is ruled out of the modern home by its separate interests. One way is to give each family member his or her own television, so that every one, apart from the rest, may listen and look, say and do nothing.

Family is no longer a career, and neither is community life. Intimacy within the family is losing ground steadily. Yet the inner demand for intimacy remains, and modern man still expects to have his marriage and his home his one haven of intimacy. It is the one place he can have intimacy without threatening his security in a heartless and impersonal work-a-day world.

Facing an accentuated need for personal intimacy in a world of anonymity, modern man turns to his wife and family to provide it. And for those at the dating stage of life, the usual expectation is that one's future wife or husband will provide adequately for the need of such intimacy. This is one of the great basic compulsions for marriage as well as the key to its success or failure. The break-up of the modern family reveals both how intense the need is and how ill-equipped man is to live with it when it is attained. Before we take up the reasons for conflict and crisis in personal intimacy, we will consider the essential conditions for achieving intimacy in marriage.

The Conditions Essential to Intimacy

We have already suggested that knowledge and understanding between persons are conditions for achieving personal intimacy. If there is to be mutual love and trust between two persons in marriage, then each must understandingly enter into the other's life. More than this, there must be responsible commitment to each other, and this commitment must be maintained by true inner fidelity. For it is one thing to take on responsibility for another person in marriage, and another thing to fulfill it with true fidelity.

A husband and wife commit themselves to the responsibilities of marriage in a covenant of love, trust, and fidelity. Each one takes on the needs of the other in an essential identification of purpose. Each one gets under the burdens of the other, accepting whatever is or is to come in the life of the other. Whether it be disappointment, sorrow, or rejection, they two have settled their mutual commitment, and each can count on the other. Whatever the cost involved in fulfilling the life of the other, or in fulfilling the potential of their life together it is accepted in a covenant of mutual concern and responsibility.

This is, of course, a hazardous undertaking, for fidelity to another person is not indigenous to sinful human nature. It has been pointed out by others that man's capacity for faithfulness makes marriage possible, while his sinful propensity for unfaithfulness makes marriage necessary.

Faithfulness undergirds and sustains marriage; marriage, conversely, places definite boundaries around personal love, making it a commitment, and encouraging faithfulness. But love is not immune from failure and betrayal. Sin in the heart is such that a person can quite readily redirect his affections in an attempt to find self-fulfillment in someone other than his marriage partner. In countless instances this goes no farther than a fantasy-lover in one's imagination. But even fantasies have a reality of their own, and infidelity in the mind and imagination can have the same moral quality as its real-life counterpart. Only an adequate love can set one free to become truly responsible for and faithful to another person both in heart and in daily life. The love and fidelity that root in an individual's relation to Christ will make the difference between the inadequacy of "I love me and want you because you make me happy," and the adequacy of "I love you and want you to be happy whatever it may cost me."

If as we have seen, personal intimacy demands a responsible commitment supported by fidelity, then love must be more than merely an emotion. For one thing, purposeful willing is at its core. Love must be willing to be committed. But then only love can afford to be concerned enough to take on and be faithful to the responsibilities of marriage. This precludes the possibility of just "falling in love." One does not simply fall into a definite willingness to assume responsibility and to sacrifice for another, especially over an indefinite period of time. Nor does one "fall" into a state of earnestly caring for another based on an intimate knowledge of that one's needs. One cannot fall into intimate knowledge of anything or anyone. Responsibility and fidelity do not just happen!

Now, to be truly responsible for another person in marriage, and to maintain fidelity to that one both in heart and in life, one must have the capacity for caring deeply. The capacity to love is the capacity to care; the two can be equated. There is really no such thing as loving apart from caring. Mature love is the ability to care intensely about someone. Romantic love by itself is necessarily devoid of the capacity for caring. Romantic love cannot be the sturdy thing that supports marriage.

Love adequate to sustain marriage is a genuine concern reaching out creatively to fulfill the needs of another. Love is the most powerful creative force in human relations. The creativeness of love is best seen at Calvary, where God wrought out the redemption of sinful man through suffering love and costly sacrifice. Love creates as it gives itself to and for the beloved. Love does not give something apart from itself; it gives itself. One who is unwilling to give cannot care, and one who does not care cannot truly give. As ungiven love is unfulfilled love, so an ungiven self is an unfulfilled self. Loving is the fulfilling of selfhood. So the capacity to love is the capacity both to care and to give; it is indeed a costly thing! Only love would choose to render itself vulnerable to the extent of losing its life for the life of the beloved.

To experience the redemptive love of God is to have every relationship in one's life profoundly altered. Marriage provides the most perfect human relationship of mutuality where the costliness of caring and giving can find its highest expression. Quite truly, marriage is said to be the school where man can learn the high cost of loving.

The Illusion of Romantic Love

This is not the place for a full discussion of romantic love, but it is the place to relate romantic intimacy to genuine personal intimacy. They are not one and the same thing, although young lovers quite generally assume them to be.

Romantic intimacy is largely the emotional unity two persons feel in their strong attraction to each other. This emotional unity can be felt intensely despite very little knowledge of each other. Personal intimacy is very different, for it requires a true knowledge and a deep caring in order that love might fulfill itself in the other person.

Romantic love is superficial and needs only an intense emotional involvement for it to thrive. So it is unable to enter sympathetically into the needs of another, and much less to desire to be a part of those needs. It is deceptive, however, for emotional unity gives a false assurance of intimacy when in fact the only bond between the two is that of romantic desire for each other. Romantic involvement is the quickest and easiest way for two persons to think that personal intimacy has been achieved. It is not difficult to understand why this should be, for romantic intimacy comes to full strength almost immediately and is very intense from its beginning. It is the intensity that makes it so deceiving. But romantic intimacy has little relation to the facts of either person's life, for it does not depend upon knowledge, but only upon the obvious attractiveness of each to the other. No wonder romantic intimacy is frequently seen to undergo a sudden collapse, breaking off as suddenly as it arose in the beginning.

It is a common illusion of young people in the throes of romantic intimacy to suppose that because their intimacy came swiftly and easily, so a complete personal intimacy in marriage will also come just as swiftly and easily. When it does not, both are hurt and sometimes convinced that they made a mistake in marrying.

Sometimes the inability to achieve intimacy at other levels of personal interaction, or even fear of such inability, will cause a young couple compulsively to accentuate their romantic intimacy, looking to it for reassurance that complete personal intimacy is being achieved when it is not at all. Is it any wonder that romantic intimacy alone is characterized by anxiety and insecurity, perplexity and jealousy? Romantic intimacy is no guarantee at all that two persons are capable of achieving the complete personal intimacy that is required in successful marriage.

In the early days of marriage, any romantic intimacy that has been carried over from courtship will soon dissolve in the multiplicity of routine involvements. Husband and wife are quickly introduced to the necessary transition from predominant involvement with each other to preoccupation with such other things as work, home, finance, children, social demands, and generally with the plain hard work of getting along in the world as a family unit. Romantic intimacy is soon shattered by routine and responsibility, and then personal intimacy must find a more solid foundation if it is to survive the realities of life together. Disappointment and disillusionment will surely come and take their rightful place within the marriage relation. These threatening invaders can be managed only as there is a real and tested ground of complete intimacy.

We have scarcely scratched the surface yet it is already plain to see that intimacy is inseparable from conflict in human relations. Other values rise up to challenge the impulse toward intimacy. Love that cares cannot rest short of achieving true and complete intimacy, but love must reckon with the fact that such intimacy in marriage will also create conflict and tension. With knowledge and caring comes the sharp issue of personal differences and the ensuing conflict. Sooner or later such conflict will reach the proportions of a personal crisis.

To be married is to expose oneself to the scrutiny of another who has married with exaggerated expectations. As it is true that in personality one must face his existing inner conflicts if he is to have a chance for real inner integration, so also in marriage husband and wife must face their existing conflicts if their marriage is to achieve real integration and intimacy. It must be recognized that marriage, more than any other human relationship, provides a better opportunity for inner fears and hostilities to be vented. No person is always lovable or loving, and just as spiritual life has its ebb and flow, so married life will also. Martin Luther commented: "What a lot of trouble there is in marriage! Think of all the squabbles Adam and Eve must have had in nine hundred years of married life!" (And how often Eve must have said to Adam: "You ate the apple!"; only to have Adam retort: "Yes, well YOU gave it to me!")

Each sex possesses advantages over the other, because each possesses that which the other does not have and yet needs. The danger is that whoever has the momentary advantage may exploit it for some subtle reason, and thus break the bond between them.

The situations are countless. Listen to the businessman as he whispers to the anonymous soul sitting next to him in the bleachers at the ball park: "I never see night games; it is easier to sneak away from the office than from my wife." Or hear the wife who is going on and on while her husband beats a retreat behind his newspaper: ". . . and it isn't your secretary I'm jealous of; it's her salary!"

Extrovertive and introvertive personalities will have no small adjustments to make. Or when one marriage partner comes from a background of affection and security, while the other comes from a home where there was quarreling and continually disruptive conflict, it will not be easy to take a realistic view of their differences and maintain equilibrium. Differences in temperament can create very great problems also. ("Is he temperamental! 90 per cent temper, and 10 per cent mental!") And there will be some whose emotional stability is easily overturned, and whose way of expressing their general need for reassurance keeps the marriage a constant "cross word puzzle" (the opposite of kind word!). Or perhaps it will be the husband whose words are sometimes sharp because he has to get them in edgewise! For the majority perhaps there will be just the problem of differences in tastes, codes, or family ritual.

"Yes," I answered you last night; "No," I say to you today. Colors seen by candlelight do not look the same by day.

Christian couples ought to remember that though they are sure that God has brought them together and they are meant for each other, they are not immune from conflict, nor will they be free from the many problems of marital adjustment. It is not enough simply to know and love the Lord.

Once two people have entered into the continuous intimacy of married life they must abandon all poses and disclose themselves as they really are. The game is up so far as any further major deception is concerned. Seeing each other under all circumstances will bring both of them out in their true colors. The inevitable scaling down of their estimates of each other will be a painful process in itself, bringing keen disappointment at times. Both may fight off a secret disillusionment. And it is during these critical days of adjustment that the threat of differences will loom the greatest, and temptation to repress them the strongest.

This crucial period of adjustment may reflect itself in absurd irritation over things of no consequence whatsoever, little things exaggerated out of all proportion. Or it may involve reactions very difficult to understand. For the girl so recently out of college, the adjustment may have to do with keeping house with its limited returns, its frustrating restrictions, its demand for more of her time, energy, imagination and patience than she ever conceived. How unmercifully it exposes her likes and dislikes! And the absorption of her husband in his work seems horribly cruel to her. It is hard to understand his particular type of impatience, and especially his inability to see her side of the picture. She is tempted to self-pity and resentfulness, and the feeling of "Is this what marriage was supposed to be? Is that what I made grades in college for?"

The husband in turn cannot understand the wife's exasperation at little things, her attitude toward the home he has worked hard to provide, the children who never seem to bother him as they do her. He cannot grasp why she should want to get away from the house when he looks forward through the day to his haven of peace.

How often Christian couples assume that because they know and love the Lord they will have a much easier adjustment to make. But emotional maturity is needed as is character development, and God uses conflict and burdens in marriage as a means of growth in both of these ways. No Christian couple can afford to ignore this principle of God's working in marriage.

Conflict Through Crisis

The cartoons of the American humorist, James Thurber, depict the conflict between husbands and wives in forms not so exaggerated as they may seem at first. He shows the hapless male cringing defensively before the aggressive female. He trades on the fact that there are countless situations in which husbands and wives may clash. This is true because the aspect of conflict is a common denominator in all human relations, simply accentuated in this, the most intimate of all such human relations.

Wrong views of conflict in marriage lead to equally wrong attitudes and responses. Some look on marriage as a contract where something is surrendered that may later be regained at will. Where such a view prevails, conflict in marriage is likely to be considered the sufficient ground for disregarding or even ending the contract. Others idealistically think of marriage as a state where love so fully controls that conflict cannot arise. Such a view, of course, will lead couples to be shocked at the first signs of conflict, and to make such a poor adjustment to it that further conflict naturally develops out of the first. This can lead to a hasty conclusion that the marriage was wrong in the first place.

A mature individual will come to marriage recognizing that it is bound to be incompatible in many ways, because it brings together two adult and diverse personalities. Of necessity each partner in the marriage brings to the relationship what has been his or her individual pattern of life. Common everyday behavior responses, habits, opinions and prejudices, family codes and rituals, are all part of the baggage of life accumulated from birth and now deposited in the marriage. Two distinctive personalities attempting to fuse in marriage scarcely realize that marriage is the bare beginning of a process of growth toward the ideal of oneness that only the years will be able to complete.

No couple can avoid certain disappointment and disillusionment in the early days of marriage, and only the immature and unrealistic will think it otherwise. There is wisdom in the reported answer of a Britisher who heard there were many divorces granted in America on the grounds of incompatibility: "But I thought that was the purpose of marriage!"

Incompatibility *is* one of the purposes of marriage! God has appointed conflict and burdens for lessons in spiritual growth. These are to be subservient to high and holy purposes.

In every marriage there is the existence of two opposing principles: completion and competition. Completion is always imperfect at best, while conflict from competition is continually created at the deepest levels of the personal relation. Having come to marriage with faith in their love, two persons discover that each ultimately loves himself more than the other. Conflict arises between self-devotion and devotion to the other. Two self-centered lives confront each other in the most self-revealing terms. Each challenges the other's self-love and freedom as they have never been challenged before. Basic conflict arises between the value of loving responsibility and the value of independence and self-desire. When the two values are at cross purposes, how virulent can frustrated self-love show itself to be! How violently it can react! It is a rude shock to many to discover that one cannot give up an independent, self-devoted and self-directed life merely by taking a marriage vow. The love in which they placed so much faith is seen to be inadequate in itself to transform the self and resolve the tension and conflict.

Personal intimacy achieved through close human attachment is inherently tragic because of the conjunction of two strong wills-to-power, the clash of two free and autonomous persons. There is resident in sinful human nature the tension between wanting to express outgoing love toward one's beloved, and the impulse at the same time to dominate the other for one's own selfish purposes. This disintegrating power of human egocentricity cannot be minimized. Human love is not immune from the possibility of tragic failure and betrayal. And to the degree that freedom of expression and action are primary to a person's code, one's conception of marriage is endangered. Marriage is not a device for two persons to pool their freedom and selfish interests for personal pleasure. Pleasure must ultimately come into conflict with responsibility; love, as we have seen clearly, must always care.

Personal intimacy, based as it is upon knowledge and understanding of another person, will reveal the weaknesses and inadequacies, faults and sins of two persons as no previous relationship had or could ever have done. Such intimate knowledge will bring to the surface all existing differences, exposing how short each one falls of the expectations of the other. In such intimacy each is rendered highly vulnerable to the other. The vulnerable one becomes sensitive to his own vulnerable places in the realization that the other has an advantage should there arise a desire to attack and hurt. One can never be truly hurt until one has experienced personal intimacy with another. Then to be rejected or hurt by the one who has shared that intimacy is to experience great pain and bitterness. No wonder there is such possibility of hurt in marriage, with the ability to hurt and to be hurt in direct proportion to the achievement of personal intimacy between two persons!

A power struggle can do but one thing; it will always frustrate intimacy, for it frustrates the free responses of love, and blocks the growth of caring and trusting. Marriage challenges not only the independent ways of each partner, and all individual claim to power or authority, but it challenges not only the independent ways of each partner, and all individual claim to power or authority, but it challenges the very existence of self-devotion. It is in this challenge that marriage brings disillusionment, for one will discover what the other person really is but in the same process discover what one is in himself. Such heightened self-knowledge means a scaling down of one's self-esteem, and the conflict itself will teach one that marriage at best is two imperfect persons imperfectly related.

It is all too easy to let such a disclosure turn affection into resentfulness and hostility. Pride reacts against its twofold hurt; it reacts against the realization that it is an imperfect person one is married to, and against the realization that oneself is exposed as an imperfect person who is disappointing to the other. The reaction itself can have a twofold effect, that of losing one's self-acceptance, and turning away from acceptance of the other person.

How suddenly holy wedlock can become unholy deadlock! How disheartening to find burdens where blessings were expected! It reminds one of the troubled young husband who was counselled by his minister to remember that after all, he had taken his bride for better or for worse. "Yes," he replied, "but she is worse than I took her for!"

Personal intimacy is threatened from another direction. Over-possessiveness is accompanied by unreasonable and exacting demands, and by a subtle jealousy. It is the sure sign of a dependent and insecure personality. But in marriage, for either person to assume a position of superiority in any area of their shared life is to court disaster, for the mutuality of two persons requires equality. Personal intimacy in the making is a fragile thing subject to every subtle personality response. How quickly and decisively it exposes and withdraws from any attempt at domination.

If in the early days of marriage there is a prevalent desire to have a love that cannot be threatened, there will be an attempt to avoid facing up to any differences that might possibly eventuate in open conflict. With previous experience, a young couple can hardly be expected to realize that any repression of differences may temporarily hold off conflict, but will all the while be building toward an inevitable crisis. Differences must be squarely faced and resolved or a personal crisis will surely come. Then love is severely tested and must prove itself adequate to establish a mutual respect and trust, and to set each partner free to live realistically and to handle conflict with assurance as it arises.

It is paradoxical yet true that love both produces the conditions of intimacy in which conflict will arise, and at the same time proves itself the only force adequate to transcend and transform conflict to make it the instrument of a deep and abiding intimacy.

Take a concrete case. A young couple have been married but a short time. Their engagement was rather short and now differences are surfacing which surprise and shock them. They feel they are in love and they long for a satisfying experience of married intimacy at all levels. But there is developing a strong fear lest rejection will result from the disillusionment they are beginning to experience from the disclosures of their intimacy. Will not such disclosures have a corroding effect upon their relationship of love?

Inwardly, the two are quite uncertain now whether they can achieve the kind of intimacy they set out to obtain, and at the same time live successfully with its disclosures and demands. Neither of them has ever known such intimacy before, so there is no experience to serve as a wise teacher. They are on their own.

They care for each other; this they know, for they have cared enough to have reached the present achievement of intimacy and to be troubled so by the prospect of anything threatening.

Now conflict is impending and it looks like a crisis ahead. How insecure they feel, and how unpleasant the tension that is developing although nothing outwardly indicates that their situation is perilous.

The tension and unpleasantness cannot continue to build up and threaten their marriage happiness, so each one inwardly accepts the fact that they must contain their intimacy at its present stage of development. They determine secretly not to draw any closer than they are now. In this way they expect to hold off any further tension that might arise from exposed differences. It is to be hoped that the tension already generated will also disappear, and their present differences will seem less significant.

So the two cease being realistic. They solve each conflict that could not be simply avoided by taking the course of easy appeasement. All real differences are repressed and hidden from open view. They are never discussed. Deliberately the two of them are drifting apart, all the while thinking that they are holding to a presently accomplished intimacy. Each one subconsciously justifies his action on the ground that it is saving their marriage from the conflict and unhappiness that would disrupt it altogether. They hardly realize that they have actually settled for a coexistence that is less than a love relationship.

To try to contain love and intimacy at a certain level is to let it wither and die, but this they do not recognize. Sexual intimacy continues, but little do they realize that it has become a substitute for the complete and growing personal intimacy they should be achieving. Along with this false substitute is a sense of dutifulness that also falsely assures them that they are fulfilling their marriage obligations.

Deep within this flight from the realities and costliness of intimacy is the frustrated longing for the satisfactions which only such growing intimacy can provide. Frustration and restlessness build up slowly but surely and create a type of conflict of their own. The craving for intimacy, and the frustration because it is blocked, intensify more and more in these victims of the boredom of an empty relationship.

From within these complex responses emerges a more mature realization now. They see that they have been dishonest with the facts of their life together, that the pain and threat of conflict in a growing intimacy would be less damaging and more tolerable than the pain and boredom of a relationship that is coming to mean nothing at all. Conflict is at least a sign of life and concern; boredom is a sign that the relationship is dead, that love has dried up. If intimacy is costly, loss of intimacy is even more costly! One might live with the conflict and pain of intimacy, even transcend it in love, and actually turn it into a creative force; conflict might even become an instrument of cohesion! But one cannot long live with a marriage where intimacy has been blocked and love is shrinking. Welcome the crisis that may lead to the way back into reality and into love!

Break-Through or Break-Up?

The attempted solution only made marriage a fraud and a pretense. Hypocrisy must out. Repressed feelings must explode. Realistic solutions must be found. Each has too long secretly resented and blamed the other, supposing the other to be responsible for his own inability to be himself or to express true feelings with the assurance of being accepted. Neither was able to see for a time that it was their flight from the realities of love and intimacy that was to be rightly blamed for the unhappiness that came. They both meant well in seeking to avoid crisis.

Now it is very plain. Either they must separate and divorce, since all the features of divorce are present already, or face frankly the points of conflict that were repressed. They must acknowledge the fears that led to a blocking-off of growth toward intimacy and see the frustration that brought about even more violent reactions. They must sense together that even a real love can wither and die if it is not nourished; that love is not static, but dynamic, that it cannot be contained or there will be regression.

There may be other areas for confession: perhaps the fears of rejection, or a proud independence that led to a power struggle, or a resistance against possible humiliation in having to be forgiven. Resentfulness and hostility must be faced as facts. If one has been at war with himself, and hence estranged from the other, this too must be surfaced.

From such a crisis must come an entirely new commitment, not only realistically to pay the cost of genuine intimacy, but in humility and consecration to seek the love of Christ that can transcend and transform all conflict. There must be a committed willingness to accept each other for just what each one is, a willingness also to forgive and to receive forgiveness. Then and then only can a couple begin to forge a true marriage. A new freedom created by mutual respect and trust will emerge. A new sense of belonging will relieve the tension and intimacy will begin to grow again. Through the crisis something profound will have been learned that could not have been learned in any other way, something of pity and forgiveness, something of sympathy and tenderness, something of respect and trust. Love will have come into its own!

Since the love of Christ can redeem and transform the incompleteness and imperfection of married love, the very tension and conflict that arises can serve as a spur to bring to a young couple the realization of what Christ can mean in their lives. As often as they turn to Him there will be a re-creation of the true relationship between themselves, and a new perspective gained on their differences and disappointments.

In the truest relationship, tension will reappear because competition and conflict will remain, but at the same time a oneness will increasingly establish itself at a deeper level than that on which the conflict occurs. The two will continue to create problems for each other, but in solving these problems they will help each other to grow, and they will be more completely man and woman, and more completely children of God. Love for them will never be looked upon as a "paid-up policy," but as a growing, ever-enriching experience, and that growth will take place in and through every struggle brought about by their growing intimacy.

Out of conflict, husband and wife must strengthen and fortify each other's self-esteem. It is intolerable that the resolving of conflict should ever require one or the other to "lose face." There is no such thing as a individual victory in marriage conflict. Such a victory would be the worst defeat of all. As Alexander Magoun puts it, only those who are really fighting their own feelings of inferiority will require a personal victory in married conflict. Such a one is still under the compulsion of trying to impress his beloved of something only ideally true of himself. The resolving of conflict must never leave one or the other humiliated or discouraged. It must rather leave each one with a sense of acceptance and love and trust. This is the only successful negotiation of conflict.

Nor must differences of opinion ever have to result in loss of emotional unity. A couple who are truly loving and working out their shared life never need the emotional reassurance of complete agreement; their mutuality is built upon a more solid foundation. And their learning through conflict is good preparation for the other crises that will surely come in life, the adversities and disappointments common to life. Each has come to accept the limitations of the other, and more especially the limitations of life together. Each has discovered it is just as important to relinquish the illusions about oneself as to relinquish illusions about the one he has married, in order that the real potentialities be understood and the real goals adopted.

In Christian marriage, conflict is a means employed by God to teach humility. Peter wrote: ". . . be subject one to another, and be clothed with humility: for God resisteth the proud, and giveth grace to the humble. Humble yourselves therefore under the mighty hand of God that he may exalt you in due time: Casting all your care upon him, for he careth for you" (I Peter 5:5-7). And James counselled us concerning conflict: "Confess your faults one to another, and pray one for another . . ." (James 5:16). This is the way to true humility and to an experience of outgoing love.

> The kindest and the happiest pair, will find occasion to forbear,
> And something every day they live, to pity and perhaps forgive.
> —Cowper

There is really no more wonderful way for human love to deepen than through the constant interaction of pity and forgiveness. This is the interaction of that "secret sympathy" that binds two lovers in the bond that God intended when He blessed His human creature with the gift of marriage.

Simplicity and Godly Sincerity

In his second letter to the Corinthian Christians, Paul speaks of his behavior in the world as being "in simplicity and godly sincerity." This is a beautiful description of the realistic life we have been speaking of in this chapter as the answer to conflict and disharmony.

Simplicity and godly sincerity are not marginal virtues in Christian life, not optional equipment for the Christian journey. These are central to true Christian experience. Spiritual life, if it is anything at all, must first be real and genuine, transparent, out in the open.

Modern society trains us to be subtle and sophisticated, indirect and devious, clever. We live by exaggeration and affection. We become experts at impression, masters at pretense. We can tell the truth while living the lie. And what dupes we delight to be! Just glance discerningly at the pages of advertising in some popular periodical!

We lie by the way we walk, the way we dress, the way we laugh. We lie by the inflection of our voices. Both our speech and our silence are calculated to deceive. We express emotions we do not feel, and our acted-out virtues are often our egotistical fascination with the possibility of rising momentarily to another's expectations, to dominate another's opinion by our own deceit. How seldom we seem to realize that a lie is always a liability. We prefer the world of make-believe. We take fiendish delight in playing a trick on real life as often as we can!

Contrast humility and meekness, sympathy and tenderness. Contrast what Paul termed simplicity and godly sincerity. Lowell said: "Sincerity is impossible unless it pervades the whole being, and the slightest pretense of it destroys it completely." It means that there can be no reality in marriage if there is unreality outside of marriage. Lack of genuineness in life generally will invade the marriage. There is no place for sophistication in marriage, nor really out of it.

It is not that we aren't ready enough to confess the marginal insincerities and leave the central insincerities untouched. (One might argue for the moral character of Hitler because he neither smoked nor drank!) We demand that our opinions be recognized as convictions, but Paul wrote: "Let love be without hypocrisy . . ." (Romans 12:9, ASV).

Humility is possible only to those who truly recognize and accept themselves for just what they really are. Spurgeon said that sincerity is the "willingness to know one's self and to be known." Simplicity and sincerity remove the strategies by which the proud ego seeks to maintain itself, and this is the first step toward humility. When a Christian says with Paul, "I am crucified with Christ," he consents among other things, to be crucified to all forms of affection. The game is up! Christ delivers the individual from all pretense and parade. There can be no more window dressing. He will give the individual a transparent life. And as in all of life, so particularly in the marriage relationship, Christ will make us authentic selves!

Heywood Broun once remarked facetiously that marriage is probably the best way for two people to get acquainted. He meant, of course, that it is possible for a husband and wife to spend years together and live as strangers. But we have seen in this chapter that God's provision is for a satisfying experience of personal intimacy in which all conflict is faced and managed, and in which the transcending and transforming love of Christ brings happiness and oneness.

3. ALL LOVE EXCELLING!

WE COME now to the nature of love. We have suggested already that whatever belongs to the true meaning of personal intimacy in Christian marriage derives its essence from love. When we speak of the capacity for caring, or for unselfishly giving, we are speaking of love. When we outline the essential conditions for personal intimacy such as respect and trust, commitment and fidelity, compassion and forgiveness, etc., we are thinking of what only love can accomplish.

The apparent problem stems from our knowledge that these qualities of love are ideally present in human relations but not adequately so in reality. Sinful human nature has the power to turn love inward, thereby making it something less than love. Love is always the desire to possess another individual in an intimate personal relation, but sinful human nature tends to pervert that possessive relation by exploiting it for selfish ends. There is in human experience a need for self-transcending love. This is possible, but it is something that must be acquired, not achieved; it has its source outside of the lover. And in consequence of their redemptive relationship to Christ, this self-transcending love may be experienced by Christian persons. What a wonderful possibility this is!

The distinction between love in its true essence, and the perversion of it in human experience, is brought out by two Greek words. True love is called *agape,* and is a word found frequently in the New Testament, primarily in reference to God's love. The human perversion of love is called *eros*, a word not found at all in the New Testament. Briefly noting the philosophical distinction between eros and agape, found as early as in Plato's *Symposium*, will help us differentiate the nature of God's love and human love. Then we can go on to see the possibility of self-transcending love as it is required in Christian marriage. Finally, we will see how it may be acquired through the Lordship of Christ.

Eros

Eros is any form of love that is determined by value outside of the person who is doing the loving. In eros one loves "because of . . ." (any value or combination of values that make up the attraction might complete the sentence). We love by eros that which we desire for our own completion and satisfaction. By definition, then, eros is love that is motivated by some value outside of the lover.

In the case of eros, the object of love is at the same time the source of that love; the loved object attracts and elicits the love. So in eros, love is a response to an external stimulus, response to that which arouses a person's expectation of pleasure and satisfaction in another. That attraction may be beauty, personal charm, warm friendliness, goodness, ability, or whatever. In other words, the essence of eros is that the impulse to love another is elicited by some value in the other. This is the very heart of sexual desire and romantic infatuation. In chapter six the nature of romantic infatuation will be more thoroughly investigated, and its nature as eros will be seen in its whole development. Suffice it to mention that eros is reflected in such expressions as "I fell in love," "I was smitten with love," "He's my dream."

Eros then is selfish love, love turned inward. Such love is inherently tragic; it is love perverted by sinful human nature, and made the instrument of self-devotion. It is brittle and fragile, and carries within itself the secret of its own destruction. Eros always wants something in return for its self-giving, and if frustrated may turn to hate.

Agape

Agape is not love that is grounded in any external value. Agape is pure love, and as such it does not have its source in the loved object. Agape does not love because of the lovableness of the loved one. It is unmotivated by anything outside of itself. Its motives arise wholly from within its own nature as love. It is not based on the expectation of anything in return, even acceptance of itself; it is wholly uncalculating in this respect. Agape is thus not an act of self-completion or self-satisfaction by means of another. It cannot be frustrated because it does not demand anything in return. It is pure outgoing desire to care for another. In its absolute form it denotes God's love, not human love.

In Christ God acted out His agape love towards us. He loved us, not because we were lovable, but because we needed love and because His nature is love! He acted in Christ to accept us, not because we were acceptable, but because we needed acceptance, and because love accepts!

Agape is used in the New Testament to denote God's love operative in the redeemed heart. It transcends and transforms eros, bringing a new quality altogether into human love. It is love redeemed by love! It is the love of God shed abroad in the heart by the Holy Spirit. It comes through a miracle of grace and forgiveness. It leads to the reorganization of all of the incentives in human life.

We recognize now that agape is distinguished as love for someone, not because of what he is, but in spite of his being just that, as Emil Brunner puts it. It has a truly creative quality, in fact is the highest of all creative forces in the sphere of personal relationships. The love of Christ that redeems the individual creates worth in the individual. Irrespective of human unworthiness, the love of God for man creates worth in him. As the object of the sacrifice of Christ, man is infinitely worthful.

God's love comes to man despite his undeserving nature, and that love comes with a creative purpose: to awaken in man the desire to receive and reciprocate that love. God's love creates its own response! It creates in man the capacity both to receive it and to reciprocate it.

God does not love us from a need in Himself for anything we can give Him in return. But He does love us with the matchless purpose of disposing us and enabling us to return that love, and thereby to enter into the communion of shared love. This is the highest blessing the human creature can experience. Therein he learns the incomparable value of creative love, and from his experience of God's love he learns something of what it is truly to love others. And the relationship most perfectly suited to the outworking of agape love on the human plane is marriage between Christians.

No experience of love can be any richer than the participants. The perfecting of love in marriage requires first of all that both persons know the love of God in Christ, and know what it is to love Him in return. The quality of love in marriage will reflect the quality of the spiritual lives of husband and wife, and especially will it reflect the growth of love for the Lord of all.

We have seen that agape love exists in God only as an absolute quality, in man only as a derived quality. Man experiences it only as he receives it from God. To receive it truly is to reciprocate it, and in learning to return it to God one learns to love others as well. Before leaving the matchless theme of love, let us just note a little more of the divine dimension. God's love is motivated by His will to give, to share, to bless, to create value in us. His love possesses the loved ones for the purpose of enriching their lives.

God's love comes to us both as mercy and as grace. It is mercy because it is totally undeserved, grace because it is freely given. God has revealed Himself to man as love, and that love exhibits the dimensions of mercy and grace. And if man is to receive it at all, he must receive it as mercy and grace.

In I John 4:7 it is declared: ". . . love is of God. . . ." This must be the case, for elsewhere John says: "God is love." God is the fountainhead of all love. I John 4:12 says: ". . . If we love one another, God dwelleth in us, and his love is perfected in us." Agape love is communicated to the Christian by the indwelling of God through His Holy Spirit. I John 4:16 reads: "God is love, and he that dwelleth in love dwelleth in God. . . ." The twofold secret is in the fact of God's indwelling the believer, and the believer's indwelling God. The experience of the love of God is maintained by constant communion with Him. I John 4:17 adds: "Herein is our love made perfect. . . ." Human love is transcended and transformed, "made perfect," as it finds its source in God's love.

In I John 4:7 it is stated: ". . . every one that loveth is born to God, and knoweth God." Verse 19 of the same chapter adds: "We love, because he first loved us" (ASV). So in sharing His love we love others with a truly outgoing love. Increasingly it may be our discovery that outgoing love has an infinite capacity for satisfying deep hungers within us.

Eros is motivated by "What can I get" and it gets pitifully little. Agape is motivated by "What can I give?" and it gets much in return!

We would not be realistic if we discounted eros entirely, for it exists in all human loving. It does indicate the beloved's value and that is worthy. Nor is it ever superseded; rather it is controlled and enriched by the agape that comes to order the whole relation. In Christian experience agape lifts eros to its highest potential.

Nine-Point Standard of Love

Love as the highest creative force in personal relationship is described in Paul's inspired paean of love, I Corinthians 13. Young couples who are engaged ought to read this chapter together, discussing each phrase and stating to each other whether they are prepared to commit themselves to this standard. Here is the one quality of life that can be extravagantly lavished without loss or regret, for as Browning said: "Love, I say, is the energy of life!"

The spectrum of love has nine hues, as Drummond tells us in his classic sermon. We shall but note each one in passing.

(1) "*Love suffereth long.*" That is, love is patience, the calm readiness to bear all things for the sake of the beloved. Love understands with the most profound perception, and thus can afford to wait.

(2) "*And is kind.*" That is love in action, blessing with a great sense of what it is to care, and understanding the need of the other. Kindness is tenderness in the fulfillment of need.

(3) "*Love envieth not.*" Here is love in competition with others. Love defers. As Paul said elsewhere:

"Outdo one another in love." Love does not stand upon rights. Betrayal only affords love a greater occasion to reach out in pity and concern.

(4) *"Love vaunteth not itself, is not puffed up."* Love is humility. Love is not a pride-reaction. Love hides even from itself, and waives all sense of self-satisfaction. Love is insensitive to the measure of acceptance and return it brings forth.

(5) *"Love doth not behave itself unseemly."* That is, love is courteous. Love is sensitive to trifles, cares even in little things. Nothing of the other's life is inconsequential to love.

(6) *"Love seeketh not her own."* Love is not selfish. It is not a matter of love giving up its rights, but of giving up its very life! Love fulfills itself in giving itself.

(7) *"Love is not easily provoked."* No true lover will hide behind the word "easily" either! Love is not offended for it is not self-regarding. Love is not touchy—self is, but love is not. Love is not easily ruffled. An offense against love is the hardest wound to receive, yet love will receive it! Love will sweeten what is bitter, and purify what is impure.

(8) *"Love thinketh no evil."* Love is guileless. It carries no suspicions, for it requires no defense of suspicion or jealousy.

(9) *"Love rejoiceth not in iniquity, but rejoiceth in the truth."* How transparently holy is love! How pure its motives! Love cherishes what truth can do, never what evil can do. Love is never retaliatory.

What a schoolroom God has given us in the marriage relation for the learning of these precious lessons! As Mary Wood has said: "There is an awe in love." What insight this gives to the statement of Shakespeare: "Love is not love which alters when it alteration finds."

And yet when we have said all this, love is more than the sum of all its components. It is indeed the very life of life, the life of God coming into our lives. The more we contemplate the love of Christ, the more we love. Love begets love. This makes it all very true that the one who has the least capacity actually to love another is the one who greatly fears he will not be loved. The one who has the capacity to love another is the least concerned about being loved. Herein lies the difference, as we shall see, between secure and insecure marriages.

A Many-Splendored Thing

Paul, writing to the Galatians, summarizes the full-orbed life of love. He speaks of the "fruit of the Spirit." Note, not "fruits," but "fruit." The nine elements all add up to one fruit, itself mentioned first: love.

Donald Grey Barnhouse has aptly described it in the following way: Joy is love singing. There can never be any joy apart from love; there may be enjoyment, but what a difference there is between joy and enjoyment!

Peace is love resting. There is no peace anywhere without love, for it is only love that can cast out fear, as John tells us in his first epistle.

Longsuffering is love enduring. There is nothing else in the world that will suffer long and remain kind all the while it suffers, but love.

Gentleness is love's true touch. Goodness is love's character. Faithfulness is love's habit. Meekness is love's self-forgetfulness. Self-control is love holding the reins.

So love is the sum and substance of the life that God gives. His love is life, and His life is love! He has demonstrated it in the suffering, forgiving love of Calvary, and He communicates it to us ceaselessly through the risen, exalted Christ in the heavenlies.

The Three Elements of Christian Married Love

The non-Christian marriage may have love in two dimensions; love in a Christian marriage has three dimensions. Following the twofold distinction of love as eros and agape, we must assign the first two elements to eros, and the last to agape. For the convenience of teaching, let us consider the threefold action of love in marriage.

(1) *Sexual love.* The capacity for physical passion in our human make-up is strong. Biological impulses rise from sexual need, triggered by the same physiological processes of sensual attraction which approximates the mating impulse of animals. There are differences, of course, notably the psychological aspect in human sexual attraction.

Romantic infatuation is often confined to this level of love. In itself erotic love is no more than lust. Within Christian love, physical desire and fulfillment have a true and meaningful place.

Marriage based on physical desire alone cannot last for long. This is ensured by the laws of God inscribed in our very moral natures. Lust is subject to a moral law of diminishing returns. All sensual satisfactions are subject to satiety, and satiety is easily followed by revulsion. The thing originally wanted is no longer wanted. Satisfaction has ceased at a point of fulfillment, and anything beyond that is only reacted against. That which was "loved" is subsequently hated. In erotic love the biological release brings an immediately pleasurable sensation. This sensation, having reached its climax, rapidly subsides. If it stands alone as a mere physical experience only, then with the passing of the physical value the spirit is left sadly conscious of its attachment to the impoverished impulses of the flesh. The spirit suffers emotional exhaustion, not emotional fulfillment, and can find no resource in the act for emotional rehabilitation. No value remains since the only value sought was physical. The biological was not able to satisfy the expectations of the psychological. The physical experience alone was not able to communicate knowledge or understanding, love or trust, sympathy or concern. The spiritual dignity and self-respect of each is revulsed by a sudden awareness that personal being was exploited and used as a means to a merely physical end, satisfying less than something personal, something less than love. There remains only emptiness and the lingering sense of a spiritual and personal dimension unfulfilled. God's gift of sex has been reduced to a sacrilege, when God meant it to be a sacrament of love and concern.

Erotic love is basically self-centered and subsequently self-destructive. It regards only its own gratification, and subordinates all higher qualities to that end. Thus it distorts an end into a means, and unwittingly fosters the very opposite of responsible love. The subtle motivation is selfish. Disappointment turns to resentfulness with frightening speed, and resentfulness to hatred. The disillusioned one then tends to seek the cause of the disappointment in the other rather than in oneself.

Even in Christian marriage where sexual expression is elevated to a higher plane altogether, such expression can turn to revulsion with terrifying ease when something happens to estrange the hearts and minds of those whose bodies have sought fulfillment in each other. There cannot be estrangement of heart and mind and still be oneness and satisfaction in the sexual union. Expressing sexual oneness becomes a fraud when there is no longer a total personal oneness to express through it. For never can the physical be isolated from the spiritual, as the one fortifies and sustains the other. The physical expresses and communicates the spiritual quality, while the spiritual redeems and ennobles the physical. Erotic love which seeks a once-for-all satisfaction is doomed to most certain disappointment.

(2) *Personal love.* It is possible for non-Christian husbands and wives to achieve a high degree of personal love and intimacy. This is still eros inasmuch as it is love motivated by value outside of the lover. It will normally include a strong physical attraction, but it rises above the merely physical to blend with it a larger personal basis for union. It is eros inasmuch as it is love by attraction, love that is grounded in the personal qualities of the other. It is usually a complex of qualities all of which add up to a total attraction. Personal love for each other is kindled in just the same way as sexual desire is kindled for each other; one desires to have as a part of himself what he finds attractive in the other. It is largely possessiveness for self-satisfaction still. It can include, however, much compatibility, affection, and self-giving consideration.

Personal love stands halfway between erotic love and Christian love. While it is essentially eros, there is something of an outgoing agape quality about it too. Still in all, the outgoing quality is not free from selfish motivation. One's personal happiness and welfare are very much at the heart of even this outgoingness. It is really "pooled self-centeredness and self-concernedness," a subtle yet nonetheless real form of ego-satisfaction. "My" happiness is less identifiable simply because it is now part of "our" happiness. So we may say that personal love falls short of being adequate for the fulfillment of the high potential of Christian married love. Each one will be satisfied only so long as the other contributes his share to the total achievement of happiness.

Sometimes it is pointed out that there are instances of altruistic concern of a high order, examples of how one can love another when the other seemingly cannot contribute anything to one's happiness. But here is precisely where ego-satisfaction can be most subtle in its disguise. There are persons whose only ego-satisfaction is in dominating another personality, and who accomplish it by being good and kind, by establishing a state of dependency in which their kindness becomes indispensable to the welfare and happiness of the other. Such outgoingness is merely the satisfaction of being a benefactor, the satisfaction of feeling oneself important to another's life. It is not love.

The inadequacy of personal love is discovered the moment we realize that love is not static. It is dynamic, and as such it must either grow and mature, or it will diminish through neglect. Love is a living quality. If love is based on the value of the beloved, that value must not only remain, but increase. This is the precarious element of all personal love. Personal love has no resource outside of itself.

(3) *Christian love*. To the two elements already identified is added a third to make up Christian love in marriage. Agape love, the love of God, is available to transform human love. It finds its source outside of self and selves, transforming everything it touches. It comes to those who respond to the love of God in Christ. When a Christian couple experience the power of His love over their life together, then in their love for Him they will find their own. Their love for Christ is the bond of their oneness, the growing strength and quality of their love for each other.

In Christian married love the loved one is loved for his or her own sake, for his or her own worth in God's sight. Each partner regards the other as a person who is significant in God's plan, and who has infinite worth as a redeemed individual. The highest objective to which husband and wife are committed in their married life is that the love of Christ may find a glorious expression in their love for each other.

Christian love shifts the center from self and selves to Christ. He becomes the source and the ultimate object of the love which husband and wife now share. It is not something one shares with the other; it is something both share in together. As Peter so beautifully put it "heirs together of the grace of life. . . ."

The whole passage found in I Peter 3 is worthy of attention. Verse 7 reads: "Likewise, ye husbands, dwell with them according to knowledge, giving honour unto the wife, as unto the weaker vessel, and as being heirs together of the grace of life; that your prayers be not hindered."

The passage suggests first that mutuality is based on "knowledge," and knowledge is gained through sharing. Knowledge will enhance respect and honor and equality —"heirs together."

It is suggested, too, that such a mutual relation is necessary to the success of individual spiritual life, "that your prayers be not hindered." Prayer is at the very heart of personal spiritual life, the first thing to shrivel up and die when some major area of life is not in tune, and when there is conscious awareness of conflict, or of the selfish domination of one over the other. Two persons sharing life in the closeness of marriage cannot pray together if their relationship is wrong. So prayer-togetherness is a crucial test in Christian marriage of the essential oneness which does or does not exist. Prayer together is the medium of much self-revelation. Prayer will only accentuate any pretense or hypocrisy, or any unwillingness to face differences. In other words, prayer-togetherness is an infallible means of disclosing how well a Christian couple is handling conflict.

It is difficult to adopt a creative attitude toward one who has deliberately injured us. To move toward that one in creative forgiveness is more than expressing reconciliation. Forgiving love will make a creative attempt to cause the other one to feel that no ill feeling is held, and further that the whole occasion has stimulated a deeper mutual understanding and more sympathetic love.

Does this seem idealistic? Indeed it is to our poor human spirits. But it is not unreachable idealism for a Christian couple. Yet it involves two problems that must be met: one must be humble enough to forgive, and one must be humble enough to accept forgiveness. Forgiveness is not merely a soft attitude toward a harsh fact; forgiveness is the vital action of love, seeking to restore the harmony that has been shattered.

Forgiving love in marriage will reflect the two qualities we previously saw to be active in God's agape love toward us. His love acts as mercy because it is directed toward the undeserving, as grace because it is freely given with "no strings attached." Forgiving love in marriage must act as mercy, forgiving when there seems to be no reason to forgive. It will act as grace, forgiving freely with no guarantee demanded.

Forgiveness is a vital function of love; it is a creative means employed by love to restore and sustain, to deepen sympathetic concern. Forgiveness is love suffering, but suffering to achieve a high and holy purpose! Young couples must learn early in marriage that forgiveness is a mighty creative force in the hands of love!

When two persons are growing in their relationship to Christ, and in their experience of His redeeming grace and love, into their lives will come a humility and tenderness that they could not develop on their own. This humility and tenderness is the soil for compassion and forgiveness, so essential for the maintenance of love.

Love will never stoop to a condescending forgiveness! It will do nothing calculated to destroy the equality and intimacy of the relationship. Forgiving love will not tolerate a lowered esteem for the one who is forgiven. Forgiving love will put the matter that called for forgiveness out of mind and life. Respect and equality will always be the more deeply established by true forgiving love.

In such an atmosphere as mutual forgiveness creates, each marriage partner can afford to be himself, and truth can be freely spoken in love. Conflicts will continue to come to the surface, of course, but conflicts will not generate tension, for tension arises only when there is no movement toward resolving the conflict. All of this is beautifully put in Ephesians 4:32 "And be ye kind one to another, tenderhearted, forgiving one another, even as God for Christ's sake hath forgiven you."

Ephesians 5 is the high-water mark in the New Testament teaching concerning the relation between husbands and wives. Only two verses are directed to wives, while the remainder is directed to husbands. It is simply said that wives are to be subject to their husbands and to reverence them, but it says a lot about the kind of husbands wives are to be subject to.

Mandate to Wives

In modern America wives are little prepared to listen to Paul's word to them. This is due, however, to a partial understanding of what is said. The word to wives is like a railroad ticket with the words stamped on its face: "Not good if detached." The truth and beauty of the word to wives will be grasped as it is seen correlated with the word to husbands.

Verse 22 (RSV) reads: "Wives, be subject to your husbands, as to the Lord. For the husband is the head of the wife as Christ is the head of the church, his body. . . ." Now wives, don't bristle at this! This does not command a slave-to-tyrant relation, or anything like it! This is a principle aimed at the very highest happiness possible for wives!

After the fall God said to the woman: ". . . thy desire shall be to thy husband, and he shall rule over thee" (Genesis 3:16). This principle is repeated in I Corinthians 11, Colossians 3, I Peter 3, and in Ephesians 5. Actually as we shall see, the wife is "subject to" and "reverences" God through her husband as the appointed head. This is vastly different from an arbitrary, independent authority which a husband might presume to exercise. He is not hereby given the prerogatove to rule with a rod of iron (or a rod of irony either!). Nor may he impose his own selfish will, and thus overshadow his wife with his own ego-satisfactions. Rather, the wife is subject to one who is to seek so to give himself in love for her as to raise her into the fulness of every blessing which he himself enjoys, and which it is possible for her to experience too. He gives himself up to the obedient search for God's will, in order that he might fulfill God's best in her life. He rules her for Christ, and he rules in the love that Christ supplies.

It has been wisely remarked that an obedient wife rules her husband. This doesn't mean, I'm sure, that the husband lays down the law and the wife makes the amendments! Rather, a wife's loving obedience will create the desire in the husband's heart to rule her only in love that cares.

Ephesians 5 states the principle of complete mutuality between husband and wife. This is first a mutuality of respect. Wives must fulfill their proper place and function if the husbands are to respect them. Husbands must fulfill their love and headship if wives are to respect them and be subject to them. Paul presupposes this when he says: "Let the husband render unto the wife due benevolence: and likewise also the wife unto the husband" (I Corinthians 7:3).

The subordination of the wife is not that of compulsion and fear; rather it originates in her freedom and love. This means, too, that such subordination can only be maintained as her freedom and love is maintained. So it is in the husband's hands! Should her freedom and love be destroyed, so will her ability to be subject to her husband.

Christ was willingly and lovingly subject to the Father; likewise the husband is to be subject to Christ, and the wife to her husband. In other words, the husband rules the wife from his own position of subjection to Christ. This precludes the possibility of the wife's subjection being degrading, for it is actually subjection to God, only to God through her husband. This exalts rather than degrades her! It is a far cry from subjection to the whims and fancies of a selfish, unreasonable, and arbitrary husband. It is subjection to one who is himself also subject to another, even God, and whose responsibility to rule his wife in love and dignity he must one day answer for.

Ephesians 5:33 reads: ". . . and the wife see that she reverence her husband." Does this mean husband-worship? ("She *must* worship him; she places burnt-offerings before him each morning!")

The meaning of this word is simply that the wife is to recognize and esteem her husband's place as the head of the family, directly under Christ the Lord of all. This is all that it means, but this is a lot!

Mandate to Husbands

Ephesians 5:25-33 is addressed to husbands, and forms a singularly complete word to husbands in New Testament instruction. Here is the other half of the exhortation to married partners which provides the key to understanding the spiritual dynamics of Christian married love.

The husband is to take the initiative in love; he is made responsible for married love. He is the lover. The command is: "Husbands, love your wives." One will seek in vain to find such a command for wives! It never says: "Wives, love your husbands." Some would suppose that this is unnecessary because husbands are such lovable fellows anyway! But hardly!

Rather, the whole mystery of creative and reciprocal love is embodied in this principle. It is the logical counterpart in marriage to the love relation between Christ and the believer. It is love creating its own response. In loving his wife, the husband causes her to love him in return.

This design of God is not meant to be reversed. Whenever the wife must be the one who initiates love and the husband only reciprocates, there is a deep fault in the relationship, sufficient in fact to bring it to an end.

Paul proceeds to set forth just exactly how husbands are to love their wives. It is "as Christ loved the church." Amazing! What loftier ideal could ever be put before husbands! The fulness of Christ's love for the church suggests five major characteristics for husbands to emulate by the power of the indwelling Holy Spirit:

(1) Christ loved the church *realistically*. He was under no illusions when He sought us in love! It was not a romantic sentiment that moved the Son of God to love us. John does not say: "For God so felt a sentiment of love toward us that He gave His only begotten Son. . . ." No! He knew us just as we were: sinful, unlovable, and unresponding. Our only capacity for love was to direct it to ourselves. But "while we were yet sinners Christ died for us"—in love! His love was not prompt-

ed by anything in us at all. And of equal significance, neither was His love for us diminished or withheld by anything in us! Our need and inability only added a quality of depth and utter self-giving to that love.

Husbands, then, must love their wives realistically. This but confirms what we saw clearly as we analyzed the conditions for achieving personal intimacy, especially as it related to the crisis which arises when differences are repressed. Now we can add that none can afford to be so realistic with each other as two redeemed Christian persons who seek their love in the pattern of Christ. If this love is going to work in their lives it must be based on fact not fancy. It must embrace all of the faults and failures, the unlovely and disagreeable elements. For this Christ's love is adequate!

(2) Christ loved the church *sacrificially*. He ". . . gave himself for it" (verse 25). How costly is love! I John 3:16 reads: "Hereby perceive we the love of God, because he laid down his life for us. . . ." The supreme demonstration of the costliness of love is the acceptance by the Lord Jesus Christ of the death of Calvary! He counted the cost of love's new creation, and paid it joyfully. He gave Himself up completely to undertake what only sacrifice could accomplish. Thus did love its mighty work!

The very life of love is to spend itself for the sake of another. Yet couples will complain: "The hardest thing to give is in." It it not because they know so pitifully little of what sacrifice is? Hence how little of what love is?

There are two thoughts on the meaning of love that go together and supplement each other. One is that emphasized by Thomas Aquinas who stressed the element of giving. This is brought out as a characteristic of Christ's love for the church. It is the idea of giving in the sense that it is a willing, desiring, and doing in order to accomplish the good of the beloved. Love takes the lover out of himself and his own needs when he gives; it identifies him with the needs of the beloved. His highest happiness, then, is in the happiness of the one he has loved with such self-giving love.

Husbands must love their wives sacrificially. They must be willing to give up all that is required to fulfill the life of the beloved. This may involve giving up some of their interests, their time, their pleasures, their ambitions, their friends. It means that nothing shall have priority over their responsibility to fulfill the needs of their wives. There is no substitute for the giving of oneself! How many wives confide to marriage counsellors that their husbands give them everything but themselves. A mink coat can never substitute for a husband's love!

The very meaning of the word "sacrifice" is arresting. It comes from the Latin, and is a compound of "sacra" which means "holy," and the verb "ficio" which means "make." The word "sacrifice" originally meant "to make holy." Since it was a costly thing to accomplish redemption, and it is ever a costly thing to strive for holiness, the word has come to mean "costliness in achieving some end." How appropriate is this word, for marriage success is a costly thing, and the end is a holy end.

(3) Christ loved the church *purposefully*. His purpose was "That he might present it to himself a glorious church . . . holy and without blemish" (verse 27). The purpose of Christ is the eventual perfection of His church. To this end the Lord Jesus Christ communicates His own life of blessing and power. He leads the church in all of its growth, directs all its walk. He perfects the church's joy. He nurtures the church's life of holiness. He does His greater works through the church which is His body.

Augustine emphasized the nature of love as chiefly the desire of the lover to be one with his beloved. Love creates a void in the heart that can only be filled by the beloved. Thus the lover is ever seeking a closer union of heart and life with his beloved. In the union of the two the meaning of life and love are realized. In Christian marriage the husband is ever to seek a deepening unity with his beloved in thought, expression, and in the shared life. This he finds possible of accomplishment through the Lord Jesus Christ in whom the union is established and sustained. As another has put it so beautifully: "Husbands, thou shalt love the Lord thy God, with all thy heart, with all thy soul, with all thy mind, and thy beloved as His gift."

So it is not enough for the husband to sing: "Take my wife and let her be, consecrated Lord to Thee!" He must love her purposefully. This will take time and thought, prayer and work, patience and persistence!

(4) Christ loved the church *wilfully*. With no motivating cause outside of Himself, God willed to love us. Agape love is not an affair of the emotion only, but is an activity of the whole personality, including the will. The mind, the heart, and the will must cooperate in loving. And it is blessedly true that where there is the will to love, there will arise feelings of love as well. Very few young people seriously consider to what a large extent love is dependent upon the action of the will. Beside the emotion there must be a degree of faith, and there must be the determination of the will.

(5) Finally, Christ loved the church *absolutely*. His love for us was without limit, without condition, and without reserve! Ephesians 5:28 reads: "So ought men to love their wives as their own bodies. He that loveth his wife loveth himself." Whether or not we are quick to acknowledge it, this is the best illustration of absolute love that can accommodate our experience: our love for ourselves!

The thought here is that a husband should not neglect his wife any more than he would neglect his own body. Actually, the underlying concept of Scripture is that they are "one flesh"; the wife is part of his body! The husband cannot neglect her without neglecting part of himself. On the same principle all he does for his wife shall return in blessing upon himself.

We summarize by saying that only grace can fill the husband's heart to rule his wife in love.

The word of Paul to husbands and wives is in perfect harmony with the complementary natures of them both. It recalls a fine word by Norval Geldenhuys: "The husband finds in the wife his complement and corrective, and vice versa. Without the woman the man quite easily becomes callous, licentious, and selfish; without the man the woman's tenderness easily degenerates into weakness, her love into sentimentality. Just as the woman cannot do without the man's independence and strength, so the man requires the dependence and tenderness of the woman. Marriage is therefore founded on the nature of both."

The requirements for successful married love are very great. In this chapter we have endeavored to show that human love in itself is inadequate. Eros must be transcended and transformed by agape; human love must be infused with divine love. This is possible when two persons bring their love to Christ. Through redemption the love of God comes into human life as mercy and grace, teaching the mystery and power of forgiving love in human relations. In returning love to Christ, husband and wife find their own love purified and strengthened.

4. SEX AS SYMBOL AND SACRAMENT

THERE are two sexes, and as Reuel Howe says, "Thank God there are not more, complicated as matters are with only two!" The very fact of two sexes implies that human experience will be profoundly affected by sexual differentiation. There is a completion and unity in marriage when sex is fulfilled; there is competition and division when the sexual function given for fulfillment becomes instead the instrument of deprivation and exploitation.

What a confused matter sexuality has been through the long centuries of human history! How little even the church has to say about it today. Individual approaches to it have been varied. Some have sought the meaning in sexual experimentation, others in trying to deny themselves any sexual expression whatsoever. Some have accepted it as a biological necessity only, others have confined the meaning to its propagative function. Some have put their faith in romance as a supposedly infallible guide to sexual fulfillment, others have simply become victims of its dynamic power for personality disintegration without assigning any meaning to it whatsoever. People seem generally to sense the mystery and sanctity of sex, yet continue to exploit the pleasure, evade the responsibility, and miss the fulfillment. Sex has become our number one enigma.

The Christian view of sex is based on the Biblical view of man as a creature made in the image of God.

He is an animal with biological functions, but he is more. He is a spiritual being. When he relates himself to God, even the most fundamental biological functions are endowed with new meanings and values, and the whole personality is involved in its entirety. The biological function of eating can have social implications, and the biological function of sex can have psychological, social, and spiritual implications. Actually, the problem of sex is not primarily moral, or social, or biological, or even psychological; it is spiritual. The Bible treats it not as something to be integrated into personality, but as a function of personality for the fulfillment of spiritual purposes. Sex is thus a symbolic expression of other values beside sex. For one thing, it expresses the desire of two persons to share their lives completely in a mutual commitment of love and trust in marriage.

The distinctive thing about the Christian concept of sex is in thus fully acknowledging it as a biological function in man, but at the same time insisting that it is a function of the total personality which at its highest level is spiritual. Its physical aspects cannot be dissociated from its spiritual aspects.

Each one of us lives in the world as a being related to other persons and things. The Christian interpretation of life is that persons are to be loved and respected, things are to be used. This is God's order in creation, and only tragic consequences can follow when we reverse the order by loving things and using persons.

A person is used instead of loved when another takes advantage of some function of that person, sex for example, to serve his own purposes alone. In so doing he values what the person can do more than what he is, thus reducing him to the status of a thing. This is the essence of prostitution. The damage is not so much what is done to the body, but what is done to the personality. For sexual intercourse is an act which affects the whole personality, a personal encounter between a man and a woman in the depths of their being, which does something permanent to each, for good or for ill. Hence it cannot be treated merely as a sensual indulgence the effects of which pass with the act.

When the sexual act is put on the basis that regards the person as a person, it must not only regard him for what he is in himself, but also for what he means to God. Sex must be part of loving another person for what that person is in himself, for what he is to God, and for what God's grace may make of that one. Sex must not in any way detract from what the other is, or counter what God intends that other shall become. Therefore sex must be retained in its proper place as God has intended it, or it becomes sin against God. Sexual sin must be seen not only as sin against the other person, but against God who gave the dignity to the one whose dignity has been violated. As Norman Pittenger has aptly put it: "It is precisely because man's sexuality may be the means to highest fulfillment that it can also be the means to lowest degradation."

The Biblical view of sex is based on the premise that man is a sinner, and that in his sex life as in other areas of his life he stands in need of God's fogiving love and transforming grace. His sex life must be redeemed and redirected according to the purposes of God. Sex is to be understood as a part of human relatedness. Nowhere do spirit and flesh so closely meet as in sexuality. Unless sex is made creative by God's grace, it will be a disintegrating force in human relatedness. Sex is good when it is regulated by God in its proper place, and when it serves the fulfillment of man as a total being.

A Christian view of sexual relationship implies an interrelatedness of persons in their total being in such a way that both function and being are preserved and honored together. In this sense the sexual union of

Christian married persons is sacramental, for it is an outward sign of an inner commitment of love which is recognized as a gift from God. Sexual intercourse is more than a physical act; it is the symbol of a spiritual relationship and the expression of the complete oneness of two persons in married love. It is the sacramental expression of the union of husband and wife, the means by which they are confirmed and nourished in that union. Sex is sacramental in that a spiritual gift and knowledge emerge through a physical act.

We need go no farther in our study of love, sex, and marriage to sense that sex needs marriage, and marriage needs sex. The two are interdependent in the design of God. Sex enhances marriage by giving it a meaning and value it would not otherwise have. Marriage likewise gives sex a meaning and value and stability it would not otherwise have. Sex without marriage is devoid of spiritual or personal meaning, is insecure and transient, exploitative and irresponsible. Marriage without sex is an incomplete relationship, a union lacking an indispensable resource for the establishment and maintenance of oneness.

Marriage is a vocation, and sex a gift. We cannot overemphasize this fact. If sex were merely a fact of nature, man would be in bondage to it. But sex is a gift of God, and so must be made subject to man's freedom and sense of responsibility toward the God who gave the gift. As a gift, sex is to be used according to the purpose of the Giver. We have a God-given right to use God's gifts, it is true, but freedom is not an irresponsible thing. Freedom demands that we use God's gifts according to His purpose; to use them in any other way is to deny and lose our freedom.

Now if sex is a gift of God, good and holy, it cannot be a regrettable overplus of guilty desire which marriage helps us to dispose of secretly! Nor does it require any justification for its existence apart from its own nature and function. Certainly the fact of propagation cannot itself justify something that otherwise would be not good! Sex is justified for what it is in itself, a medium of expression and unification in marriage. Perhaps this is as proper a place as any to add that sexual intercourse in marriage is a means of expressing and communicating the deepest feelings and assurances of love and commitment of the whole life to another, and this in a medium more flexible and profound than speech.

Of the many false notions relating to the fact of sex is the idea that a superior and spiritual love will not require physical intimacy, indeed is wholly separated from such expressions of a physical nature. This notion is compatible with the concept of the body as something inferior, the vehicle of sin but not of grace. But if sex is a gift of God, even as the body itself is a sacred trust from God, a vehicle of grace as well as of sin, then it is not a superior or spiritual love that denies all physical expression. It is rather a lack in love, an unwillingness to take seriously the physical needs of the partner, a rejection of the gift of God. It is for this very reason that Paul called continence a fraud. He also taught in I Corinthians 7:4 that "The wife hath not power of her own body, but the husband: and likewise also the husband hath not power of his own body, but the wife." Each has a right to the physical fulfillment of love which is found in physical intimacy.

The Bible views the body as the vehicle for the expression of spiritual values. Thus sex cannot be separated from the love which gives it true meaning. Human married love has a proper place for sexual desire and fulfillment. It differs from lust in that it is the desire to fully interact with the other person as a person, as an object of love and care, not as a convenient thing to satisfy one's indulgence.

It is increasingly clear that the Biblical view of sex is constructed on the principle of oneness in the marriage relation. Sexual intercourse is the physical establishment and confirmation of that oneness. The true dignity of sex is in its ability to enhance this personal unity between two persons who have committed themselves to each other in love and marriage. In sexual intercourse the couple becomes joined in an indissoluble unity, called in the Bible "one flesh." This oneness is exclusive for it establishes a unity which is complete, and into which no other person can enter or add anything. In this union there are greater creative possibilities than could be achieved by them as separate individuals, and since sexual union enhances the larger achievement of creativeness, it is dignified as an instrument of creativeness. When sex does not participate in married creativeness it loses its meaning and becomes instead a degrading thing.

In coming together sexually, a man and woman either affirm or deny all that sexual intercourse is meant to be. They either affirm the fulfillment of love and mutual commitment in an abiding union, or they enact a parody of marriage which can only result in the disintegration of personality and the ultimate collapse of the relation. It will leave only a sense of emptiness and of the misuse and squandering of a gift of God.

The right use of sexual intercourse is a means of glorifying God in the body, as Paul exhorts us to do in I Corinthians 6:19. In true marriage oneness the gift of intercourse is offered to God in thanksgiving, and thereby it attains its true beauty and meaning. As Derrick Sherwin Bailey has written: "The sexual acts will always be either a joyful affirmation of their common life, or a revelation of its defects."

As a husband and wife transcend their self-love, and truly love each other, sex expresses responsible love and care. The sexual impulse is stabilized and transformed into a creative energy, whereas outside of permanent marriage it tends to be a destructive force in its effect upon the higher life of man. Outside of marriage sex becomes a destructive passion which separates persons because it makes use of another for a selfish end; it is exploitative, and the relation is parasitic.

The spiritual dynamics of sex require that we regard it as dedicated to objectives other than mere self-satisfaction, and as related to God, to love, to marriage, and to society. These four relations are either blessed or blighted by sex insofar as sex is or is not the fulfillment of the divine purpose.

So sexual union can never be considered as "making love," for the meeting of two bodies cannot make love. It can only enrich and express love that is already present between two persons. The quality of the sexual experience will depend upon the quality of the love and oneness that it expresses. For whether they realize it or not, married persons come together sexually to express the whole meaning and quality of their relationship. Their sexual union is a most searching test of what their whole marriage means to them. When their fellowship and communion together is warm and strong, nothing hindering their sense of oneness, then they are drawn to each other sexually in search of fulfillment. When their oneness and communion is impaired, when there is a sense of emotional distance between them, their sexual interest will tend to wither away or become fraudulent.

We can conclude then that sex is not sinful in itself, but may indeed become sinful because of the way in which it can gather together and bring into abuse so many dimensions of personality, the relationship with God, and the relationship with others of His children. Sex outside of marriage is sinful because it violates

God's holy purpose of establishing full and permanent oneness between two persons sealed by the sexual union.

In the Bible the word "know" is used as a synonym for sexual intercourse. This is not an evasion of direct language, as though the matter were too delicate to speak of. The Bible is not known for squeamishness. Rather, there is in the use of the word "know" a profound disclosure of the nature of the sexual relation. It most accurately describes what psychology has only recently discerned.

Through the sexual relation in marriage one discovers something of another being and thus something of himself, that he had not known before. The unity of the flesh consists in the fact that two persons have mutually revealed to each other the inner secret of their bodily being, as Otto Piper terms it, and now by means of this knowledge they are inseparably bound together in an exclusive relationship. Man as husband thus reveals to a woman the secret of her womanhood; woman as wife reveals to a man the secret of his manhood. Each discovers the harmony of his being in the oneness of the marriage relation, especially and uniquely as it is sealed in the expression of "one flesh" through sexual intercourse. Thus in a singular way sex in marriage reveals something of the depth of meaning of another person, of oneself, and of the possible relation between two persons. This proper use of sex establishes a sense of belonging through knowing and sharing that is deep and profound.

If a person does not order his sex life according to this purpose, then he meets the other person with only a part of himself, and in consequence there is no true fulfillment. He neither knows nor loves the other fully, nor does he let the other fully know and love him by knowing. We have seen repeatedly that love is dependent upon an experience of knowing the other person, and this is now seen to be true in the matter of the sexual expression of love.

Two extremes deserve notice: many couples expect too much of sex in marriage, and many expect too little. Both are unfortunate and damaging extremes. First, let us take the case of a couple who expect too much of sex in marriage.

Sexual intercourse can never bring complete satisfaction between two persons. Nor can a couple fully express their mutual love through sexual intimacy alone. It is a mistake to think that love only requires this expression. Sexual intimacy enhances other expressions of love and tenderness and care, but it is not a substitute for other expressions of love or for other values in marriage.

Take the case of those who expect too little of sex in marriage. For them it is only the experience of physical satisfaction. But to them it must become something more; it must become the symbol of their whole relationship, the unique and profound symbol of full personal understanding and oneness. It must express something of the depths of communion possible where self-life has been surrendered for the sake of the fulfillment of the life of the other. Coming freely and unashamedly, each unveils both body and soul to the other, accepting the other for just what that one is in himself. Each partner finds in the communion of flesh and spirit a personal re-creation, a confident sense of well-being and self-respect. Both body and soul have been selflessly yielded to each other, and there is nothing regretted. The highest within the individual has been accounted for, oneness has been expressed, yet individuality has not been harmed.

In such an experience there is an assured sense that every adjustment and crisis can be met together in the same unique oneness. The disappointments that are inseparably a part of human sexual fellowship shall not be cause for offense or emotional disunity, for the love in which the two have met is sufficient to transcend all disappointment. Sexual intercourse, as fragile and brittle as it may be, is thus dignified by the fact that Christian love is able to utilize every form of human relatedness, including this, for blessing and recreation. When it is love that is sincerely expressed through sexual intercourse, the quality of the experience does not depend at all upon perfect technique. An overemphasis upon technique only points up a lack of insight into what it is that sexual intimacy symbolizes.

We have stressed up to this point the place of sex in marriage as symbol and sacrament. We have noted that sex is meaningful in and of itself, as a part of human relatedness in love. Following the best of Protestant writers, we have said that sex does not require justification by any of its possible consequences such as propagation. It is here that Protestant Biblical interpretation finds its widest divergence from Roman Catholic thought.

As Otto Piper points out with convincing force, parenthood can enrich marriage, but it cannot establish or sustain it. Sexual desire can never be equated with the desire to have children. It is not the desire to have children that stimulates sexual desire. If it were otherwise we would naturally expect either Jesus or Paul to have some word prohibiting sexual intercourse in marriage in cases where propagation were impossible or where it was not the intention of the marriage partners. But this is not to be found. The Bible regards procreation as one of the attendant blessings and functions, but not the only or the primary function. As Derrick Sherwin Bailey so aptly puts it: "Intercourse may imply the possibility of procreation, but it means the certainty of union in one flesh."

However, with the emphasis placed on sex as symbol and sacrament, we must not neglect the vital procreative function. Sex is our link to the past and future as well as the cement of our present. As Harry Kruener has said pointedly: "In the mystery of sex is hidden the mystery of new life, and only the most shallow soul can be careless before that mystery."

To sum up the purposes inherent in normal sexual experience within Christian marriage, let us briefly note four distinct aspects.

(1) Biologically, tensions are released through ecstatic pleasure and satisfaction. This is the least of the values, but not to be depreciated, for the pleasure is God-given too. It is a mistake to think that the pleasure is a sinful aspect.

(2) Socially, the meaning and dignity of one's own body is discovered, and that of another person, in this relationship in which each accepts the other as truly and fully as one accepts himself. The body is discerned to be part of the whole personality, a vehicle for self-giving and for imparting blessing to another, an instrument in the fulfillment of another's whole personality. Sex in marriage is an indispensable part of the complete relation between husband and wife, and is thus a social force.

(3) Psychologically, there is a sense of fulfillment and security. The values of interdependence are uniquely brought home to husband and wife in their sexual intimacy. They understand something of the mystery of how love and understanding are reciprocated by means of sexual intercourse.

(4) Spiritually, the unique union and communion between husband and wife are discovered to represent the same spiritual meaning and mystery as the union and communion of the trusting sinner and the gracious Redeemer. The oneness established in marriage is symbol

of the oneness between the individual and God through redemption.

It is upon the basis of the principles discussed above that Christians believe that sexual intercourse in marriage is but another function of life that comes within the pale of what Paul meant when he wrote: ". . . whatsoever ye do, do all to the glory of God" (I Corinthians 10:31). It is one way in which Christian couples can fulfill the other injunction of Paul to glorify God in the body as well as in the spirit which are His.

Before bringing this chapter to a close, perhaps a practical word will be helpful to some who read. Often Christians approach the counsellor with the fear that there is a sexual incompatibility. They point to frustrations and lack of sexual fulfillment in their early days of marriage. Sometimes there is desperation about it. So-called sexual incompatibility is psychological incompatibility, provided the two persons are normally structured. Sometimes it is a matter of ignorance about the fundamental facts of sex. Other times it is an ignorance of God's gift and how it is to be received with thanksgiving, its use offered up to Him in gratitude. Beyond this it is a matter of patiently growing in sensitivity one to the other, discerning with increasing ability the other's needs and how those needs can best be met. It is a matter, too, of compromising with the other until harmonious fulfillment is achieved. This takes time and thoughtfulness and affection. Above all there seems to be need for young couples to realize that life's many demands must not be allowed to crowd their sex life into the hours of fatigue and disinterest. Many Christian couples are guilty of being so occupied with living as to leave no time for loving.

5. FAMILY-PLANNING FACTORS

QUITE appropriately it has been said that "babies are the coupons attached to the bonds of matrimony." Dr. Otto Piper calls them "blessed burdens!" What a privilege it is for married couples to build their homes around such a central joy and responsibility as the children whom God has given. Is there another responsibility in life that can compare with that of parenthood? In every well-ordered marriage the number one concern ought to be family-planning. Planned parenthood is a vocation under God and as such it necessitates a spiritual and intelligent consideration of birth control. It sometimes necessitates a consideration of infertility and its possible correction, or of sterility and its attendant question of whether to adopt children. These are vital matters to be taken up in this chapter.

One of the golden themes running through Scripture is that of God's promises to parents and their children. God has graciously entered into convenant relationship with believing parents and their children. Formal establishment of a covenant community began with Abraham. That covenant community was first a family, then a nation of families, showing that the unit of God's concern is not the individual but the family. At that time circumcision was given as a seal of the covenant, performed not only upon the male parent but upon the male children as well, signifying that the covenant blessing rested upon the family.

Quite interestingly, except for the command in the first chapter of Genesis to multiply and replenish the earth, there is no development of the theme of procreation in the Bible. In fact, while Jesus and Paul both talk about marriage and divorce, neither is recorded as saying a word about the duty of parenthood as such! Yet the whole Bible breathes the high privilege, the essential duty, and the continuing responsibilities of parenthood.

In the spiritual life, union of the believer with Christ is meant to issue in fruitfulness. Christian virtues are the fruit of such vital union. Evangelism follows the same principle: God gives spiritual birth, but redeemed men and women are the instruments He uses. In the same manner the marriage union is meant to issue in fruitfulness. A couple's vital union is objectified by those living representations outside of themselves, their children. The children's existence accentuates the parents' sense of the permanency of their marriage and of their inviolable oneness. The very blend of traits in the children, traits derived from both parents, accords the parents new understanding of their complementary oneness. A married couple may violate and renounce their oneness, but they can never remove the extension of that oneness in their children.

God employs the relation between parents and children as a means of grace in the lives of both. As the parental relation is a vehicle of sin, the sinful nature and ways being transmitted to the offspring, so the parental relation is intended to be a means of grace, a vehicle for transmitting the redemptive grace of God. Parents are given children in sacred trust, to train them spiritually, especially to lead them to Christ. Thus the home is to be a church within the church. Parents are privileged to covenant their children to God, and to claim God's blessing upon their children insofar as they, the parents, are faithful in fulfilling their terms of the covenant.

The home on earth is to pattern after and reflect the household of God. The relation of parents to children should reflect that of the Heavenly Father to His redeemed children. The love which only parents can know, and the joy which follows the achievements of the children, tell in a profound way of God's love and joy with respect to His children. The heartaches and deep concerns which parents have for the welfare and waywardness of their children remind them of God's heart-interest in His own. The discipline necessary for molding the wills of growing children will speak to parents of the discipline the Heavenly Father must exercise toward them. Yes, there can be no higher prerogative in marriage than to bring children into the world, and train them for God, providing all things necessary for them according to the resources God gives. To rear children for time and for eternity is the highest possible mission in life!

But what of those who cannot have children of their own? Infertility may or may not indicate sterility. If the inability to produce a fertilized ovum is discovered to be a problem of infertility, there are medical corrections that can be made. In our society infertility is a very real and widespread problem, but fortunately much can be done about it. Sometimes it requires a team of specialists. An endocrinologist and sometimes a psychiatrist are called in. For the man a urologist, for the woman a gynecologist, will probably be brought into the case study. If the inability is permanently caused by either husband or wife, it is a problem of sterility. A conservative estimate (Dr. Overstreet reports as high as 17 per cent) is that one of every ten couples who want children is unable to have them. Two hundred couples apply for every child available for adoption. Only 33 per cent of infertile husbands and wives are being helped. More and more it is being found that in our complex society emotional factors play a determinative role.

For a Christian couple it is not enough to assume that since God has not given children it is not His will that they should have children. They ought to seek medical advice to determine any possible problem of infertility. Where infertility is indicated, proper treatment should then be undertaken. For those with limited means the Planned Parenthood Federation of America will provide counsel and direction, with cost scaled according to family income. Where sterility is definitely indicated, the couple should turn their prayer-interest to the possibility of adopting children.

Adoption provides a Christian home for children who need a home and who are available for legal adoption. Many children need such homes but are not available for legal adoption. To provide a Christian foster home for such children is a blessed ministry, but may involve complications far beyond those encountered when a child may be legally adopted. The legal status should be ascertained at the very beginning.

Adoption is also a means of achieving happiness for those who cannot have children of their own. A Christian home opened to children in need is more than a Christian kindness; it is a high form of personal evangelism. To mold a life for God is a profound privilege, whether that life be given to a couple by God through birth or adoption. In either case the child is a sacred trust from God. In marriage God creates a home and family unit, so that He is honored when childless couples take a responsible concern for children in need of a family where they will be loved and cared for and accepted as members with full family privileges. In fact, such children have a right to belong to Christian homes! This is one phase of positive Christian family-planning!

Christians who do not want children, and so are unwilling either to have their own or to adopt others, are morally immature or selfishly unyielded to God to the point that marriage for them is wrong. In sharp contrast, what precious spiritual lessons and joys await those who learn to love and care for children not their own but put in their trust by God!

Adoption can be arranged through (1) an approved adoption agency, (2) the children's department of a local welfare authority, (3) through a third party such as a doctor or lawyer, or (4) directly through the mother or legal guardian of the child. The first two are the only methods recommended unqualifiedly. Agencies take every care to fit the child to the new home, to secure legal protection, to put every professional service to work to make for a successful adoption in every way. Before a child is made available for adoption, the parents are given time to fully settle their decision. The child is examined by physicians and psychologists; case histories and mental tests are made. Should a child later prove to be defective, the agency is prepared to take the child back, whereas an individual most likely would not. In the heartbreak of such returns, agencies often can ease the process of detachment by providing another child to which the love and care can be transferred. Persons who let out their child without legal adoptive procedures may easily change their minds and successfully move to regain the child. What heartbreak is encountered by the would-be adoptive parents!

One should beware of any person, whether lawyer or doctor, who promises to get you a child quickly and with no questions asked. One should also know what the total fee may be should a child be gotten through such a third person. Even pastors with good intentions may be unwittingly instrumental in arranging a direct adoptive procedure which lacks legal protection, only to see the matter hopelessly complicated for years to come, or suddenly terminated without any legal recourse. Any couple thinking of adoption would do well to write to the U.S. Children's Bureau, Washington, D.C., for Publication 331 entitled "Essentials of Adoption Law and Procedure." If resources seem limited locally for making application for adoption, information can be secured through the Child Welfare League of America, or through the Children's Division of the Department of Public Welfare of your state.

Sometimes several children from one family are left and every effort is made to keep them together. It is possible to adopt more than one at the same time. Of course, understandably most couples apply for an infant so that they may have the joy of rearing a little one through all the stages, thus helping to shape that personality from the very start. Children orphaned at later stages often are not taken. But there can be advantages in adopting an older child. Hereditary defects are more readily detected, often childhood diseases are past, testing results are more reliable, and personality traits are more easily discerned.

Shall Christian couples pass by these children for selfish reasons? When there is no apparent success in securing an infant for adoption, may it not indicate that it is within the will of God that a couple take an older child? Especially if the couple themselves are older, say thirty-five and beyond, there may be a more desirable age difference between themselves and the older child.

An older child usually visits the prospective parents until both he and they feel ready for him to stay permanently. The procedure is appropriately different from that of placing an infant. The trial period which must precede legal adoption in any case makes it possible to judge the satisfactory adjustment being made. In the case of a child being adopted from an agency, a professionally qualified case worker will visit frequently in order to observe the total adjustment and to make any proper recommendations.

There is a tendency for those desirous of adopting a child to become irritated and discouraged by the length of time required for their application to produce results. They complain about the "red tape" involved. Such couples should recognize that it is better to have the "red tape" before adoption than afterward. They should also be glad that the natural parents or guardians are given ample time to settle their decision, so that when a child is given to the agency, all claims are relinquished. And as Frances Lockridge puts it: "Prospective foster parents . . . want the agency to do in a week what it would take them nine months to do themselves." Despite the seeming delays, there are thousands of adoptions in our country each year. And the number is not likely to decrease.

When a child is adopted, he is to be loved for his own sake alone, as an end in himself, and not merely as a means of providing happiness for the adoptive parents. Still less must the child be used to cover a couple's self-conscious infertility, or for diverting attention from other weaknesses in their marriage. It certainly ought never to be a couple's desire to adopt a child on the premise that a failing or faltering marriage will be saved by the addition of a child! Here again an agency is best employed since the case worker will likely detect any false motives of this nature, either assisting in their correction or steering the couple away from the idea of adoption at that time. A Christian couple will pray realistically about their motives and goals in adopting a child, and will determine to have a love for the child akin to the love they themselves have received from the One who loves them for themselves alone.

Christian faith delights in the incredible fact that God has adopted sinners into His family, having loved the unlovable, redeeming them without cause outside of Himself and His strong love, and granting His redeemed children all the rights and privileges of the divine inheritance. In like manner, the Christian couple should provide for their adopted children all the rights and privileges that a natural-born child of their own would have. When a child is gotten through an approved agency this will be legally secured.

Will it be difficult to tell a child he is adopted? Or should it be kept from him? Most adoption agencies, upon the basis of sound experience, insist that the child be told by the new parents just as soon as he is able to understand. The important thing is how the child is told. Better that he find our directly and in the proper way, than to find out through a careless relative or when the parent is caught unprepared. The wise and loving parent can make this knowledge an actual reinforcement of the child's feeling of security. He can generally explain that the child's real parents could not provide as nice a home as they wanted him to have, and because they loved him so they were willing to give him up although it was hard for them to do so. The Christian adoptive parents can further explain that after they had prayed about God's will for their family, God chose that he should come into their home, instead of giving them their own child by birth. After praying and searching for the best child, the one who could make their home the happiest, they chose him from all the rest. So he is a very special answer to prayer and to their greatest desire!

Wayne Oates reverently calls our attention to "the Heavenly Father who adopted His own Son out to a Palestinian maid and her husband." Surely, providing a Christian home for adopted children must be very close to the heart of God!

Perhaps the most urgent question in the area of family-planning is that of birth control. We may settle it that scientific contraception and the dissemination of birth control information is here and here to stay. It is something to be squarely faced, spiritually reasoned, and fearlessly discussed among Christian young people. For at last the size of a family may be determined by choice rather than by chance, and once an idea like this is loose in the world, it can never be recalled. It may be impeded by prejudice and authority, whether of legal or religious origin, but it cannot be halted. Like television, for good or ill, it is here to stay. Like nuclear science, for creative or destructive ends, it is something the world will live with from now on. And to decry it as ungodly, regardless of the use to which it is put, will cut little ice with a generation of college-trained young people who want hard facts and clear reasoning. As Dr. Karl Menninger in an article, "Psychiatric Aspects of Contraception," writes: "A deliberate program of enforced attitudes, backed up by pious references to the will of God, accomplishes its results only at the expense of inner conflict and real suffering." This is the attitude responsible for the modern Mother Goose Rhyme that goes something like this:

There was an old woman who lived in a shoe;
She had so many children because she didn't know what to do.

In justice to both bride and groom, but particularly to the bride, policy regarding birth control should be mutually understood before the wedding, or preferably even before the engagement is announced. It is a gross oversimplification to say that this question relates merely to a couple's selfish desire. Here rather is an issue deeply rooted in the patterns of family life and changing society, its ramifications touching every phase of human life and interest.

World sociology warns that the world population problem is becoming acute. Emil Brunner points out that in 1800 Europe's population was reckoned to be about 160 million, whereas today it has risen to about 460 million. Infant mortality used to be so great that on the average only a third of all children survived. A mother needed to bear six children in order to maintain the population. Today three births per mother are considered adequate for this purpose. Children today are an increasing economic burden and an increasing personal burden. They are supported by parents for a longer period than formerly, and tend to be mouths to feed rather than hands to work. Children do not contribute to family maintenance as they did in former generations, so they put a drain upon the family standard of living rather than contributing to it. Men and women are less willing to have large families which limit their freedom and opportunity to enjoy what modern life holds out to them. Knowledge and demand combine to further the movement for family-planning by birth limitation and spacing. The world picture is far different today than in that early dawn of human history when God said to Adam and Eve in their uninhabited earth: "Be fruitful and multiply." Nor should that command be construed to suggest that each woman must bear the total limit of children physically possible—quite an unwarranted assumption!

We are not dealing with a matter of expedience, but of Christian morality. With both scientific information and advanced moral theory at hand today, a responsible Christian couple dare not drift unthinkingly either into the practice or avoidance of birth planning. Ideally, controlled conception in order to limit and space births is one aspect of intelligent human aspiration to serve the best interests of family life and society at large, women and children in particular.

The term "birth control" is not altogether satisfactory, for it tends to convey the idea that science has mastered a technique of absolute control of conception, and this is not the case. To others it has suggested a synonym for abortion or sterilization. But in abortion a new individual life is destroyed, and in sterilization conception is rendered permanently impossible. Birth control differs in being a relative limitation of conception which can be terminated at will. Technically, the term "birth control" denotes the positive as well as the negative aspects of family-planning. It concerns not merely birth prevention, but also the timing and spacing of births. This accords with such recent clinical research as that of the National Committee on Maternal Health which reports that, when births are one year apart, the loss of babies is nearly 50 per cent higher than when the births are two years apart. So the movement has more to do with planning than prevention!

It was because of these confusing ideas that in 1942 the National Birth Control League was renamed the Planned Parenthood Federation of America. This new name emphasizes the fact that birth control is aimed at encouraging responsible married persons to become parents. Perhaps the movement is best described as voluntary and responsible parenthood. For a working definition the following should serve: "Birth control is a measure used voluntarily by responsible married persons to limit births to those which are desired, and to space them to the best advantage of parents and child."

Birth control is not to be looked upon, then, as an end in itself, but simply as a means—and then not only as a means of limiting births, but of protecting other values open to the couple and to their family and society. If in other things care and planning are intelligent and right, why not in the most important event in human life, the birth of a child? Ray Baber cites a cartoon by Lichty that illustrates the point. A married young man is explaining to another about their new baby: "Yes, he's a planned baby all right. When we learned he was coming we gave up our plans for a vacation and a new car." Joseph Fletcher pointedly suggests that parenthood is made for man, not man for parenthood.

For centuries the question of birth control was studied as part of the problem of population control. Although birth control methods have been practiced for nearly as long as history is recorded, the medical approach to contraception has been quite recent. Sociology and psychology are rather recent branches of social science that have advanced the study and theory of birth control along with a few pioneer individuals such as Francis Place in England (1825-1850), Charles Knowlton and George Drysdale in America. Contraceptive practices had begun to spread in Germany, France, and England despite the fact that these pioneers ventured alone and unaided upon an organized attempt to educate the masses. The medical profession until very recently did not assist the program of planned parenthood because of the moral controversy involving church authority both Catholic and Protestant, and probably also for the reason that the profession was more concerned with the affirmation of life rather than its denial. The failure of the medical profession to accept leadership in this remarkable social revolution is unfortunately a factor in the rocket-like rise of commercial dissemination of opinion which has not infrequently been of an antisocial nature.

The career of Margaret Sanger is well known. The change in attitude toward birth control in America is graphically portrayed by two pictures hanging on the wall of the Margaret Sanger Research Bureau in New York City. One, taken in 1917, shows Margaret Sanger being sentenced to jail for providing contraceptive information to women in the first birth control clinic established in the United States. The second picture, taken in 1949, shows her receiving an honorary degree from Smith College as a "leader in the world-wide study of population problems, and pioneer in the American birth control movement."

Actually, the science of procreation has made notable progress only within the past thirty years. The science of eugenics is the counterstudy to contraception, concerned with improvement in human breeding. It is another phase of the profession that provides means on the one hand whereby conception may be controlled, and on the other whereby some marriages otherwise childless may now be fruitful.

Medical summaries dating from 1936 show that medical opinion was rapidly changing at that time in the direction of the new view held in western European countries. Today there are legalized clinics in forty-one states and the District of Columbia, nearly half sponsored by state health departments. Only two states are holdouts, still legally prohibiting the dissemination of birth control information. They are the dominantly Roman Catholic states of Massachusetts and Connecticut.

Presently the first Planned Parenthood Research Professorship is being established at the Medical Center of the University of Kansas. This may seem incredible in view of other medical advances, but until recently not a single medical school assisted the program of planned parenthood. Conflict of authority, both legal and religious, had kept medical progress in a stalemate. As late as 1947, a survey of approximately one-third of the physicians in the country conducted by Dr. Alan F. Guttmacher of Johns Hopkins University School of Medicine revealed that three-fourths of all physicians had received no medical instruction in contraception.

There is not a single Biblical reference to guide us in this matter, the reference to Onan being entirely irrelevant. It is left a matter of individual conscience, but not without certain principles to point the way. Whatever the method of birth limitation, the question of motive is foremost. Is the motive birth prevention or birth planning? Prevention indicates irresponsibility; planning indicates responsibility. And when a person says, "I believe in planned families," if that one is a Christian, the first implication is that of prayer-planned families. It seems as wrong for a Christian couple to have children without praying and planning according to their understanding of God's will, as not to have children without praying.

There are those who say: "I have faith to believe that God will not allow conception except when He wants us to have children." Is this faith, or naïveté, or blind selfishness? Does the married partner share the same faith? Does such faith include perfect willingness to have a large family with births following in close succession? Are the two willing and prepared to accept responsibility for how many children come? These are questions that must be answered with wholehearted affirmation if one is to exercise such a "faith" principle.

It is difficult, if not impossible, to maintain logically that God will set aside the laws of fertility and conception in behalf of those who desire to indulge an unregulated, unprayed-about sex life. It would be difficult to believe that conception is an act of divine providence alone when, throughout all the rest of human experience, the law of cause and effect obtains. Actually, if one were to argue that children are invariably the gift of

God, given only as He wills a couple to have them, how must one explain the coming of children out of wedlock? Are the children of illicit unions the appointed gifts of God to those unions? Can we simply give way to the drives within our natures and not expect the natural consequences? To hold to this is to contradict the fact that all desires and drives in human life are controllable by knowledge and will. We cannot ignore the basic fact that all birth control is ultimately one or another form of self-control. Self-control, however implemented, is a Christian virtue, one of the nine fruits of the Spirit according to Galatians 5:23 (RSV).

Those who seem not to plan their families are generally those with large families. Actually they have planned it this way, for an unplanned sexual relationship is a plan of a sort; it is a deliberate course of action taken with the consequences clearly in view. Incredible as this may seem to many, this plan is chosen by some couples despite their understanding that by overbreeding they are sentencing themselves to poverty and parental hardship, and their children to underprivileged home and community life. Some ignorantly assume a fatalistic attitude toward the outcome of their sexual relationship. With others it is simply the assuming that their only choice is between having many children and abstaining from one of the chief pleasures of their existence. Still others have children they cannot adequately support because they find in a large family the compensations they do not find elsewhere in society. If we were to probe further we would discover many psychological factors operating among those of lower economic levels to cause them to be indifferent or even hostile to the opportunities afforded them to have birth control information and assistance.

In our complex society, one of the persistent maladjustments brought to the marriage counsellor is that of the young couple who resent the fact that the wife became pregnant the first week of their marriage. This resentment rises from the desire to accomplish marital adjustment without the complications associated with pregnancy. The husband and wife would rather concentrate upon their own relationship without the necessity of immediately having to prepare for the coming of a child. Young people facing long educational careers do not want to postpone marriage unnecessarily, yet do not feel they can manage if they are to have a child in the first year or two. Economically they may be unprepared, especially if the wife must work to help her husband through school. They claim a right to have safeguards when such safeguards are available. Not that they desire to prevent having a family, but only to postpone it for good reasons at present.

By contraceptive knowledge, those who would protect the sexual act and family establishment from qualitatively inferior values remove the danger of an unwanted pregnancy. What could more seriously cloud the whole sexual relation than an unwanted pregnancy for which the couple is not prepared emotionally, economically or otherwise? By the same principle, couples who believe they have honestly met their responsibility to God in having the children they can properly rear, will certainly not find increasing satisfaction nor the fulfillment of oneness in an act which constantly endangers their sense of responsibility for those whom they care about.

Dr. Karl Menninger rightly reasons: "There are certainly some women who are well enough to have sexual intercourse but not well enough to bear children, and it would seem to me that the health of such women should be safeguarded without forcing them to be continent and without forcing their husbands to choose between continence and adultery. There are other women who cannot bring healthy children into the world and it would seem obvious that they should not be obliged or even permitted to bring unhealthy children into the world."

With man, reproduction is not simply a necessity of the species, but a personal decision. It is not a matter of chance, but choice. Whatever the method, restricting conception involves the application of knowledge and will. The charge is sometimes levelled against contraception as though it were the exclusive means of limiting births, but this will not hold. We have noted that there are three other methods. As Dean James Pike has commented, even clerical celibacy prevents the coming of children into the world. The moral question is only between what some term "natural" methods of birth control, and so-called "artificial" methods. Since there are more ways than one, a brief evaluation of each will help us determine which is most acceptable.

1. *Abstinence.* Since the Christian view is that sex expresses the love, the commitment, and the mutual fulfillment of two married persons, abstinence is contrary to the design of God for marriage, and thus ethically wrong. Paul flatly calls abstinence on the part of one partner in a marriage "fraud" (I Corinthians 7:3-5). Permanent abstinence is maintained usually by those who loath the sexual act to begin with and are immature to the extent that they should not be married. Authorities are divided, some insisting that the evidence is inconclusive that abstinence is harmful, but the majority declaring that continence extended over a long period is unwise. It is said to be a detrimental influence upon normal sexual experience, a cause for psychological depression and conflict, an incentive to vice, and a source of risk to domestic compatibility. Periodic continence over short periods of time seems entirely proper and in

accord with personal well-being. This method we shall consider next.

2. *The "rhythm" method.* This method restricts intercourse to the period in the woman's menstrual cycle when ovulation most probably will not take place. Some Catholic and Protestant writers are overenthusiastic about the safety of the "safe period" (i.e. Norval Geldenhuys, "The Intimate Life"), whereas most medical authorities state that there are too many variables not yet fully determined. Perhaps the most conservative statement is that of Hartman who suggests that the best evidence now at hand points to a mid-interval ovulation as a rule for the human species. We may be close, but we are not yet certain of the individual woman's time of ovulation.

If sexual intercourse is looked upon as the fulfillment of a recurring need within the lives of married persons, such fulfillment should be correlated with the desire of the partners. However, unless it were possible to correlate sexual fulfillment with peaks of desire and the woman's infertile period, the use of the "rhythm" method would rob the woman of proper fulfillment when desire may be greatest.

3. *Coitus interruptus.* Withdrawal before orgasm is perhaps the oldest and most common method used. Reliability rates low for the reason that the method presupposes more control than can normally be counted upon. There is not always precise control of orgasm or full awareness of the moment of ejaculation. As to the psychological effects, the sense of oneness is lost when withdrawal robs the couple of the closest embrace at the height of coitus. Sexual satisfaction is diminished considerably with the constant anxiety which attends such a necessity for withdrawal in the nick of time.

4. *Contraceptive devices.* The issue is drawn at this point, the charge being levelled that "artificial" devices

unnaturally interfere with fertilization. It is not a question of what is socially detrimental, but of what is morally wrong. On one side, it is held that periodic continence during the fertile period is ethical because it involves no interference with the normal processes of nature. Nature herself is regarded as responsible for the nonappearance of pregnancy. Those on the other side of the debate recognize no essential difference between methods used since the result is the same, but believe that contraceptives are less harmful physically and psychologically, more reliable, and less likely to interfere with sexual satisfaction than periodic continence. Of course it must be recognized that some contraceptives are harmful, so that proper methods must be prescribed by a reliable physican.

Nearly all Roman Catholics, and not a few Protestants, still hold that any interference with natural processes is interference with the providence of God, such interference being sinful regardless of the motivation. Contraception is regarded as a deviation from an essential order of creation, especially because it concerns the possible life of an individual. Those who take this position generally allow at least a qualified use of the "rhythm" method on the ground that it is not interference with nature, but cooperation with it.

Let us grant that scientific contraception is a form of interference with nature. Is not civilization replete with means of interfering with nature, most of which we depend upon and take for granted in our day-by-day living? Pasteurization is an interference with nature; the "natural" thing would be for babies to drink milk that contained germs and for a certain percentage of those babies to die of milk-borne disease. Vaccination is an interference with nature. So is a haircut! So is the use of soap! Man is constantly intervening in the course of nature and environment. His very dignity is his God-given ability to govern nature and make it serve higher purposes in the human enterprise!

Man is called to a high vocation as a free moral agent. He may share the creative processes of God and thus enhance the values of those creative processes. God has given to man both intelligence and the way of divine guidance as means of entering into partnership with God in the fulfillment of His highest purposes in the world. Nature's principles and possibilities are combined with man and his intelligent direction from God to fulfill God's perfect will. Both man's freedom and his rationality presuppose God's design that man should be sovereign over nature. Were it not for man's sinfulness, this sovereignty would be very great indeed. But now in a world spoiled by sin this sovereignty is a struggle of mind and act. Nonetheless, freedom and rationaltiy make man responsible to God for all his acts. Whether man lets nature take its course, or interferes intelligently and morally to achieve better ends, is itself a decision for which man shall be responsible to God. In every possibility which comes before him, man must make a moral decision as to which responsible course of action he shall take, and which ends shall be served, the constructive or destructive. Christians must ever pray that God will guide them in bringing the discoveries of human progress under the dominion of God's sovereign grace and purpose. And let it be remembered that the dedicated science that has provided the knowledge and techniques of contraception by interfering with nature is the same that has reduced infant mortality, and has also made it possible for many to have children in what otherwise would be childless marriages—both by interfering with nature!

It is argued that dissemination of birth control information and availability of contraceptives leads to promiscuous sexual behavior and the degrading of public morals. But it is always a poor argument that blames knowledge for behavior. For most advances in human knowledge can be turned to constructive or destructive ends. All privilege creates responsibility and the danger of sinful solicitation. It is part of knowledge and morality to discern the right ends and employ them. So far as contraception is concerned, it is the duty of moral and spiritual education to make know the right ends and to assist in their accomplishment. It is by the right use of such knowledge that sincere young couples are enabled to enter into marriage without the fear of added responsibility before they are ready, lessening marriage postponement and the possibility of subsequent illicit relationships. Perhaps the more real danger is that couples may postpone having children indefinitely because their standard of living rises with their income, and they continue to justify such postponement.

The most important pronouncement reflecting the new attitude of Protestantism appeared in 1931 in the report of the Committee on Marriage and the Home of the Federal Council of Churches of Christ in America. It consisted of a majority declaration of approval of the use of contraceptives. While the liberal elements of Protestantism have been in the foreranks in this change of theological opinion, it would be a mistake to associate the shift in thought with the more radical departures from evangelical theology. The author has had occasion to poll highly regarded leaders in evangelical ranks across America on this question. It would seem that in all wings of the church there is an accelerating acceptance of scientific contraception as a part of responsible Christian parenthood.

In "Ideals in Medicine, a Christian Approach to Medical Practice," issued in 1958 by the Christian Medical Fellowship of Great Britain, the authors state: "Clearly it is the wife who most needs the benefits of family planning. On the one hand unplanned pregnancies may be an intolerable burden, and the child may suffer in consequence, while on the other, without the security of adequate contraception, she may not enjoy the proper satisfactions of her marital relationship. For the Christian, the use of contraceptives is a matter for the individual conscience." The same authors declare: "It is difficult, in logic and on the grounds of Christian principle, to reject the use of contraceptives, and yet to allow that it is right to take advantage of the 'safe period.' " Increasingly the judgment of Christian authorities follows that of Dietrich Bonhoeffer: "But it must be frankly admitted that in principle there is no difference between the various methods which reason may choose to apply."

The excellent statement of the Clergymen's Advisory Committee of the Planned Parenthood Federation says in part: "Parenthood is an experience which is even more significantly spiritual than physical. Therefore we believe that parents should participate in purposive planning for procreation. It is a child's right to come into the world as planned-for and wanted. Both of these factors will enhance the high and sacred meanings of family life. . . . Every married couple should decide in a sense of vocation under God whether they ought at a given time to increase the size of their family. It is every child's birthright to be reared by parents who feel that parenthood is a voluntary sharing in God's creativity."

It is generally held that we do not yet have an ideal method of contraception. The ideal would seem to be a tablet taken orally. American scientists are at work in the field of steroid hormones dispensed in tablet form to be taken orally, which if successful would offer the simplest of all contraceptives and a method devoid of the psychological disadvantages which accompany the use of all others so far developed. Compounds presently being studied are progestins, synthetic substitutes for the natural hormone, progesterone, that all women secrete during pregnancy and known to prevent further ovulation during that time.

Presently the best advice is for a couple to consult their family physician at the time of the premarital examination. He will advise the contraceptive best adapted to the individual, and will make the proper adaptation. It has been suggested that the method used should be under the control of the woman in order that she may be assured that the necessary care has been taken, since she is the one most directly affected by the calculated risk involved. But in a marriage of loyal life-partnership and love, the responsibility of either one should be acceptable should science discover that either one or the other offers the best anatomical or physiological condition for contraceptive success.

Henry Bowman's criteria for choosing a contraceptive are sound: (1) it should be relatively effective; (2) it should be relatively easy to use, simple, and readily understood; (3) it should be readily available and relatively inexpensive; (4) it should be aesthetically acceptable to both parties and repugnant to neither; (5) it should permit normal satisfactory and successful sexual adjustment; (6) it should have no harmful results (no chemical or mechanical irritant that may give rise to infection or poisoning); and (7) it should be temporary, in the sense that its use may be terminated at will.

Bowman's last-mentioned condition is an important one. The decision to use a contraceptive is a once-at-a-time decision, having to do with a particular time, not with the whole future. It is an answer to the question: "What is the will of God in this matter at this time?" Contraception is a vocational choice that concerns a couple's present ability to have and care for a child properly.

For a couple to believe that it is the will of God for them to have a child at a given time and to prevent it by any means (abstinence, rhythm, or contraceptive) is sinful. But if the two prayerfully agree that their conviction of God's will is that they do not have a child at that time, then they have a positive duty to use whatever means is best to ensure the fulfillment of that conviction. So it may be concluded that any or all means may be right if subject to the prayerful understanding of both persons as to God's will for them; but any means will be wrong if not subject to such prayerful seeking of God's will. The first requisite is that the will of the couple be aligned with the will of God insofar as they can ascertain that will through prayer, discussion, and a humble walk with the Lord.

The family on earth ought to mirror in every way the family above. The love and security the Christian experiences in Christ must extend to every relation in the earthly family life. There is no higher privilege than to be a Christian parent, and there could be no higher motivation in life than to prepare in every possible way to be a worthy Christian parent.

PART II

PROBLEMS IN CHRISTIAN COURTSHIP

6. INFATUATION: FACTS AND FICTIONS

ONE of the four questions most frequently asked by young people in discussions having to do with dating or marriage, according to Dr. Oliver Butterfield and others, is "How can I know when I am really in love?" The purposes of this chapter are to investigate the nature of romantic infatuation, and to contrast infatuation with love. For simplicity we will identify infatuation with romantic love, although some would prefer to find some distinction. Admittedly, we can only speak of tendencies and general characteristics, for it is not possible arbitrarily to draw lines and say: "Love is always like this, while infatuation is always like that." The distinctions are not perfectly distinct!

Romantic love has a very real place in the development of true married love, but infatuation does not. Romantic love is first romantic infatuation, but it has a place as it becomes less and less a part of infatuation, and more and more a true and abiding quality in the couple's relationship. What we are saying is that infatuation may be the start of a real love when the first spell of excitement transfers over into something genuine. So we cannot be too rigid in drawing contrasts, recognizing that infatuation can evolve into love, and that it is a mighty difficult task to say just when it becomes no longer infatuation but is now love. There are no simple rules or neat little formulas that can take the place of emotional maturity and sound judgment when an individual must evaluate his own experience of involvement with a person of the opposite sex. Each situation is as unique and distinct as the lives of the two persons who make a part of it.

It must be noted that young people confront the need for making the distinction between romantic infatuation and love when they are emotionally least able to do so. The decision comes when they are caught up in a highly-charged emotional atmosphere, and are acting more on the basis of emotional compulsion than on rational judgment. How much this fact ought to call forth the sympathetic understanding of their seniors who have long since forgotten their own problems along this line!

If only one word could be said about how to recognize true love as opposed to romantic infatuation, it would have to be the common-sense word: "Wait!" Time clarifies most of life's issues and enigmas, and certainly the important issues can afford the test of time. Every romantic relationship requires the test of time, as well as the test of an occasional separation. This is a fundamental law in determining the will of God. The passing of time affords opportunity for change, growth, and experience. Surely young people for whom the choice shall determine the whole course of future years and happiness can afford these tests. As someone remarked: "It's pretty serious business choosing the ancestors of your children!" The one who chooses a wife or husband truly marries the whole family, for an entire family strain is taken on, and out of the marriage shall come a totally new strain. In distinguishing between romantic infatuation and love, one makes the greatest of decisions in life as to whether he shall limit or expand his own possibilities for personal enrichment in the years that lie ahead.

Romantic infatuation is the ground upon which is

erected America's greatest cult, the cult of romance. Its adherents number in the millions. The entertainment and advertising worlds promote the great American worship of romance. Real love has become identified with reel love. It makes up the colossal fairy story at the heart of our culture.

The fairy story is usually told something like this: "I am a very attractive and lovable person, fascinating and desirable in every way. But I managed to go unnoticed for a long time. The reason for that was that the one and only person in this universe had not come my way. There was one just made for me and for no other, and at the right moment he was to come into my life. Then suddenly he appeared! In that moment our eyes met and I knew he was for me. He was my dream, my inspiration! He had everything! He was tall, tan, and terrific! We kissed and I knew I could not live without him. This was love, because I was tingling with excitement all over. Nothing mattered now except that we were together. How could anything else be important but this? We would live only for each other in perfect bliss. If there had been any doubt, all doubt vanished when we held each other close. This is what I had longed for all my life. He made me feel so good. Love has brought me my ideal. There could be no reason to wait a moment longer. With his scintillating sense of humor I knew we would never disagree about anything. Our love for each other would hurdle all obstacles as though they were nothing. Brought together by the hand of fate, we must obey and marry before it's too late! You dare not put off love for it might die if not acted on right now." And so they married and lived happily ever after in the delightful ecstasy of married bliss!

So goes the great fairy story, and how many there are who believe it! But this is really the adolescent viewpoint on life. This is part of the make-believe world that intrigues the adolescent mind. Unfortunately, there are countless adults who have never moved from the adolescent plateau of maturity. A vast number of marriages in America are "adolescent" marriages.

While compartmentalizing always risks the criticism of arbitrariness, it is generally an aid to understanding. We shall proceed now to draw a series of contrasts between romantic infatuation and the love that sustains marriage.

(1) Romantic infatuation may happen suddenly and without warning, whereas love grows, and all growth takes time. One may "fall" into infatuation, but one cannot fall into love. Love produces a growing relationship, whereas infatuation effects little change in the relationship with the passing of time. Usually when a young person asks about love at first sight it is because he wants some reassurance of his hope that a present romantic attachment may be love, and because he is already rationalizing a premature decision based on an emotional involvement.

A person can never be sure at the time when the right one appears, for to love a person one must know that person well. This not only takes time but it takes seeing that other one in a variety of situations, under many circumstances. An individual may be infatuated on the basis of only one contact and practically no knowledge whatsoever of the other. Attraction is possible without knowledge of the personality of the other, whereas love holds itself in abeyance until the other can be known intimately and understandingly. Love is more than a fascination at first sight, more than a will-o'-the-wisp, more than an excitement in what is presently new and novel, mysterious and intriguing and inviting. Only those people who do not know each other intimately can feel romantically infatuated. Strangely, infatuated people think that love is an indefinable mystery that is nonetheless easily and infallibly identified when it hits! They regard it as an all-or-nothing kind of feeling that knows no variation of degree. In reality, love is a complex of many feelings that will differ in intensity according to the circumstances in which it is found.

So love is a true process of growth and development, like the ripening of fruit and the erecting of a building. It is subject to laws of growth and principles of development. There is nothing automatic about it. Infatuated persons think of love as something that is automatic in its working.

An individual can actually love being loved, or love the feeling of being loved, or even love the feeling of loving—and yet not be in love. Love at first sight may be merely a compulsive need finding expression in a romantic attachment. Sometimes an individual has a strong urge to love another, and this urge focuses upon the first one of the opposite sex who is normally attractive and who responds with a little affection. It is a form of sheer sentimentality, fed by all of the romantic illusions propagated in our culture. A young person so conditioned comes to expect love to be a form of exciting and thrilling adventure into a realm of mystery, secret symbolism, and exclusive association with another who must be won through subtle intrigue and conquest. Such romantic infatuation with all its ingenious ways of becoming involved can come to absorb all one's attention. It is made of the stuff of dreams, and is largely a condition of being in love with love.

A particularly romantic situation is readily transferred over mentally to the one who shared it, as though just to be with that person will always create such an atmosphere of romance at any time or place. One tends to daydream of all kinds of romantic situations in which they two figure rather sensationally. He envisions himself as the great lover, or she envisions herself as the irresistible object of attraction. Romantic infatuation makes much of sophisticated and subtle impressions, stressing glamour rather than character. Character and virtue are too prosaic for the infatuated person. The romanticist is easily offended when the object of his attentions appears in something less than romantic attire, or make-up, or even attitude. One expects the other always to be in somewhat of a romantic mood, feeling it to be a personal affront when such is not the case. Such infatuation exalts the discovery aspect of personal attraction, whereas love dwells on the value of increasingly familiar and recurring thoughts, subjects of conversation, interests and activities. Infatuation thrives on a constant round of exhilarating flattery and preoccupation with each other, insisting upon an ever-intensifying relation of emotional commitment. True love is calm and steady, and intensifies slowly but surely with the simple passing of time, and as interests and experiences are shared together.

(2) Romantic infatuation may arise from an acquaintance with only one, or at best a few, characteristics of the other person. Love grows out of an appraisal of the total personality of the other, and through exploration of all the known characteristics of the other. Love is not content to base itself on one segment of personality; rather, when a person is in love, it is love of the total personality. Feelings of love grow primarily out of the developing relationship with the other, and from a full-orbed estimate of the many facets of the other's personality and way of life. An infatuated person has intense feelings for the other person, but feelings which are quite unconnected to any growing relationship with that one. He merely attaches his self-generated emotions to his chosen object.

It is highly intolerable and generally offending for an infatuated person to feel he or she is being analyzed by the other. Such a one is subconsciously being very careful to exhibit only that side of his or her personality that is sure to be acceptable. This is felt to be certainly sufficient, and any observed or imagined analysis beyond this is highly offensive. It seems to be a disregard for one's perfectly obvious desire. Any action on the part of the other that would prompt feelings of unworthiness is resented. But love is never like this, for it wants to know and to be known, to achieve the real intimacy which comes with complete sharing and knowledge.

Love will dare to ask such questions as: "Would she be the kind of mother I would want for my children? the kind of woman I would want my friends to know well and enjoy with me? the one I could still continue to love if poor health were to take away her vitality and beauty?" Or she might ask: "Is he the kind I would want to be father of my children? the kind of man I would want to live with day in and day out? the man I want my friends and folks to know? the one with whom I could work out daily problems, or endure life's cruelest crises? Does our relationship become steadily deeper and richer?"

A person in love is willing to ask questions, to make investigations, to risk comparisons. Such a one will want to measure the sympathy each has for the other's faults, to go through emotional crises to see how they face them together. It becomes important to see the other at home, or with a work project, or among other people socially, or under stress. True love will be concerned with whatever concerns the other, whereas romantic infatuation can get along just as well when all of these matters are ignored completely.

(3) Romantic infatuation is self-centered and looks at the other as a means to an end. Love is other-centered, outgoing, releasing and investing the energies of life in joyous and spontaneous concern for the security

and well-being and growth of the other person. It will manifest a tender concern, while infatuation only makes a pose of tenderness. If one finds fulfillment of his own life in consecration to the needs and potentials of the loved one, then it is certainly not mere infatuation. For as love grows, one rethinks and replans the goals of his life with renewed ambition to find ways to give his beloved every assistance in developing a creative life of her own. There will be true spontaneity in their interaction, a naturalness that is free from affection and calculated actions. Infatuation may seem to be spontaneous, but it is only a counterfeit; it is impulse, and impulse that results from a felt need for maintaining or reassuring the relation. Impulse is always the warped expression of spontaneity that has been blocked. Love can afford to be spontaneous and natural, but infatuation cannot.

An infatuated person thinks he is living "only for the other" but this is not so at all. Actually he is living out his own desires by means of the other one. But idealistically neither can we say that the person in love is living "only for the other." Love transcends this to create mutual self-fulfillment. Love lives for the union itself, for the creative possibilities of the union. We saw it earlier: "Each for the other *and* both for Christ." But we must see if as extensive in another direction also. The union itself is capable of creative ends. Family life and children are creative goals of the union. Whereas an infatuated couple expects to find happiness, a couple in love expects to achieve it. They work for their mutual benefit, spurred by the possibilities of a creative union.

A couple in love will talk about many common interests outside themselves, which become at the same time a part of themselves. They turn their attention outward to the world they live in as well as inward to their feelings about each other. They do not merely get off by themselves; they move together into a full sharing of rich values and experiences they find outside themselves. They do not look only at each other, but they look together at the larger life around them, discovering a range of common interests, shared friendships, and challenging tasks. They face together the important problems with which human beings must cope in a mature relationship to life. They look together at all of the issues involved in taking their place responsibly in the world as a unit of two and perhaps more. They love with their minds and wills and purposes as well as with their hearts. And because they love with their minds, their emotions achieve new depth and meaning and constancy. Their love takes on a spiritual quality as they recognize their love as a gift from God. They recognize that marriage shall be an undertaking in the presence of God as well as a venture with each other. Thus an infinite dimension is added to their shared life. Love is woven into a pattern of living, and thus is begun a true and solid identification.

All of this is beyond the capacity of romantic infatuation, which is too fragile and unpredictable and irresponsible. Romantic infatuation is too preoccupied with emotional reassurance and with "how our love is making out." Infatuation is truly self-centered, but love is other-centered, and marriage is union-centered. One is ingrowing, the other outgoing. And this leads us to our next major contrast, somewhat overlapping it.

(4) An infatuated person tends to think of the other person as strangely separate from himself despite their strong emotional unity, whereas a person in love feels a true identification with the other one. Those in love seem to be a real team, not only good lovers but good partners as well. Affection becomes deep and real when they experience mutual responses in many areas, for there is actually developing a more complete union of

the real selves. There is a growing sense of what "we" think, "we" do, "we" like, "we" dream.

The infatuated person is more likely to settle for a superficial identification, for an almost immediate feeling of emotional unity arises in an infatuation. One hears, for instance, "She makes me feel I am the kind of person I wish I were." Actually such a one longs for identification, grasps at the slender thread of emotional mutuality to convince himself that it is so, and ceases looking for any other evidence. He mistakenly relies on this state of induced emotional elation as evidence of true personal identification. It is a case where emotional interdependence, proper in its place, is out of all proportion. One tries to make a part of life do for the whole of it. With nothing else to go on, it is no wonder that two persons deep in an infatuation actually desire to consume each other emotionally. One pitiful feature which seems to remain with those who have never known anything but infatuation is that they are incapable of loving, not daring to give themselves in outgoing love for fear they will be cheated out of what little emotional satisfaction they receive in these intense but short-lived infatuations.

How slender emotional unity is in itself is exhibited in how quickly it can vanish when disagreement enters into the infatuation. Hostility and withdrawal come suddenly when infatuated persons disagree. Any conflict of thought or action brings an immediate sense of threat to the whole relationship, and since infatuation demands an all-or-nothing feeling, one can suddenly decide to react against the entire affair. Anger and a breaking-off of such a relationship can be just as sudden and just as intense as was the beginning of it.

Sir Walter Scott wrote that there must be "a secret sympathy"; this requires a real identification of two persons at many levels of life. Sympathy is built upon knowledge and understanding sufficient to share the reactions of the other, to enter into the fears and anxieties, the hopes and longings of that one who has grown dear.

True identification brings self-discovery and self-fulfillment through healthy growth with and for another person. To love is to live two lives with great freedom, joy, and inspiration; it is to live one's own life and that of one's beloved. Then to share joys is to double them; to share sorrows is to halve them! This is a far superior identification to that which is mere enjoyment *of* another or *with* another. True identification will encompass intellectual life, social life, emotional life, and especially spiritual life. A constant growth toward oneness in all of these areas will be the characteristic mark.

(5) An infatuated person may be "in love" with two or more persons simultaneously, whereas genuine love centers in one person only. Any individual is capable of achieving a true love with any one of many persons who might come into his life. Most persons are perfectly capable of learning to love any one of a great number of possibilities. If the person has normal attractiveness and congeniality, if the rest of the relationship comes along satisfactorily, and especially if the two spend considerable time together in mutually desirable activities, love can grow between them. The point to be made here, however, is that love settles upon one person, and its growth relates to that one alone.

Infatuation, having no real roots, needs only a certain situation and the proper romantic props and one thinks he is in love. This can happen any number of times and it can happen with two or more persons simultaneously. Every counsellor of young people has had the experience of answering the question: "Can a person be in love with two people at the same time?" Infatuation is fickle by nature.

(6) An infatuated person tends to have a false sense of security about his love affair, which is based on wishful thinking, or sometimes upon a complusive need for reassurance. A person in love tends to have a true sense of security in his relationship, based on a growing range of trust and affection and mutual concerns. The infatuated person may actually have a sense of insecurity. It is this that usually expresses itself in possessiveness and fits of jealousy, or in unreasonable demands for exclusive rights to the time and activity of the other individual. Love, by contradistinction, is never demanding, possessive, or unreasonable.

The monotony or boredom of a prosaic existence, perhaps a drab family or job relation, may compel an individual to seek a romantic adventure, with no thought of permanence or responsible commitment or even love, but merely of excitement and for reassurance that he can command such an affair when he wants to. He thrives for the time on a situation where he is seemingly free from all other routines and responsibilities, from the burden of friends and fellow workmen and family, and where all is pure pleasure and adventure though of an unreal sort.

When one says: "I can't live without you," it is usually infatuation. (There are few corpses lying in the streets despite the high percentage of break-up among such lovers!) This is not love, but rather a sign of dependency, of a compulsive need for self-assurance, or perhaps of one's sensing that he has not developed the capactity truly to love someone else.

Romantic infatuation is more often a device for restoring one's wobbly self-assurance than many would conceive. Romance becomes for some a subconscious symbol of social success. One seems to gain status, at least in his own eyes, when he has secured an attachment with a member of the opposite sex, a status he cannot feel in himself alone. The very feeling of status, or security, is transferred in this thinking to that of love.

Normally, in the process of maturation, there are three steps. An individual should mature through the steps from childhood dependency on to adolescent independency, and then on to mature adult interdependency. Infatuation often reveals the fact that a person has stopped growing emotionally at the level of dependency. Perhaps his particular need is for maternal protection, or paternal dominance; he subconsciously seeks this in a substitute.

Lack of confidence in one's ability to love or to hold another's love is evident in yet other infatuations. Love grows because of certain principles of relationship, but infatuation can result from a variety of factors within personality itself, especially compulsive needs that arise therefrom. A man frequently will demand a loyalty he fears he has not won and does not deserve. A woman may exaggerate little offenses, like being a moment late. Yet one clings desperately to the other, compulsively seeking to have and to hold, although the experience is tempestuous and exhausting, leaving neither one the richer but only the poorer for it. This reassurance-seeking individual is the type who hugs the other passionately and whispers breathlessly: "You do love me, darling, don't you? You know you do! I'm sure you do! Don't you? Say you do!"

Again, an infatuation may result from a subconscious attempt to break out of a sense of isolation and loneliness. Such an infatuation is found in the type who says: "You are my only reason for living." Let's face it: if that is really his only reason for living then he just hasn't got an adequate reason for living!

All the types discussed are dependency relationships of one kind or another, attempts to meet certain compulsive needs by some experience of romantic infatuation. It is nothing more than a parasitic relationship, one person leeching on to someone else because of a compulsive need in oneself. No meager amount of hypocrisy will be needed to sustain such a relation. It tends rather to such motivation as: "She will know I love her if I do what she wants." One seeks to impress another by fulfilling that one's wishes, but it is only a present expedient to fortify the relationship in its present state, and really has nothing to do with true concern for the future needs of the other person. How often a woman is sure that her lover has been converted because he is so willing to follow her during their days of courtship, only to find after marriage that it was just an expedient calculated to turn the trick at the time. It is a common tragedy that love is frequently mistaken for what is only parasitic dependency! How appallingly empty life becomes when one personality is exploited because of another's need for self-assurance! The basis for such attachment is always fear and insecurity coupled with a need for reassurance and for an experience of personal intimacy.

Infatuation encourages infatuation! One takes delight in being treated as though he were perfection itself, even though it can only obscure momentarily his own dissatisfaction with himself. It is a delight to be treated as the individual which in one's fantasies about himself he would like himself to be. What more is this than a device for keeping one temporarily happy with himself?

Of course, the greater the discrepancy between the fantasy and the reality, the greater the need for outside reassurance. Infatuation may provide for such a one the thrill of: "See, I am lovable! I am an admirable and desirable person!"

Infatuation, you see, is in some instances an attempt, subconscious of course, to overcome the experiences of childhood which convinced an individual that he was unworthy, or unacceptable, or unlovable. There is an inner craving compelling one to seek such a relationship as will assure him of his worth and acceptance, that he is capable of loving and being loved. An infatuation seems to bring this reassurance.

In every romantic counterfeit of love there is a self-centered person and an irrational reassurance involved. There is never a desire to produce with the other person the conditions under which each can spontaneously and fully express his real self. This will be explored more fully under our next point where we see the conflict between reality and idealization.

(7) An individual who is infatuated sustains a mental picture of the object of his attentions. This mental image is largely an idealization. It is unsupported by and unchecked against reality. Idealization is one of the major problems in infatuation.

Persons in love also idealize to a certain extent, and to that extent it is proper and to be expected. But two differences are notable: first, the idealization is not so grandiose. Second, the idealization is checked against reality continually, and without fear or self-deception.

Infatuation, constructed as it is upon little, if any, real knowledge of the other person, must of necessity be largely idealization. One builds up a fantasy-image of another person's whole personality upon the basis of a few characteristics exhibited in a romantic situation. Idealization, once begun, blocks any attempt to know the total personality in a realistic way. The attractive points are exaggerated because this is desired. These are concentrated upon to the exclusion of all other considerations. Idealization actually replaces the other with an imaginary person with whom one imaginatively interacts. One mentally creates in the other what he wishes to find there, and then "falls in love" with the image he has created. Because one entertains the ideal of a perfect mate (to suit his own perfection!), and wishes with all his might that it could be realized in this present object of attention, one tends to project perfection where the facts do not warrant it. That same individual would probably admit rationally that there are no more perfect loves than there are perfect persons, and that there are no perfect persons, and still will let idealization dominate his attachment. This delightful dream-world is sustained so long as is possible. The pleasures seem to outweigh the advantages of a rational and realistic appraisal, and the benefit of a sound footing to the relationship.

Those who love are more realistic, and less concerned with idealizations that cannot possibly be embodied in daily life. True love is rather ruthless when it comes to make-believe, whereas infatuation thrives on it. Love is not blind! But infatuation is blind in one eye, and thoroughly enjoys this partial blindness!

Romantic love may rise above pure infatuation and often does. To do so it must face realities in a more mature way, and be no longer content with enchanted castles, but rather with bread and taxes. It will properly align itself as it becomes concerned with the hard business of working out a devoted partnership, and realizes that no one can live very long with an idealized image!

When idealization dominates the relation, absence makes the heart grow fonder for the simple reason that the real person's presence gives way to the imaginary one, and one craves the idealized image which grows as a fantasy in his mind. In true love, absence makes the heart grow fonder for the reason that the couple has established a solid ground of mutual affection and trust and interests, and the realization of what they have together is only enhanced by separation. Short separations are advisable for all couples in order that they may be objective and seek to determine whether or not their attachment is based on idealization or on love.

There are many marks of an idealized image. For example, if he claims, "She's my inspiration" or she exclaims, "He's my dreamboat!" it is probably a highly idealized image and not the real article. Or, if on the basis of a single exciting contact, she states: "I feel as though I have known him all my life!" one may well suspect that she sees in the appearance and actions of a certain individual a dearly loved father, or uncle, or friend, and thus idealizes the person. Anyone who bears a remote resemblance to a dear one may be the target for idealization, and consequently for an infatuation of a particular type.

Two interesting effects of idealization are possible, one of which will invariably come about. Having idealized another, one may idealize himself. Everything then is projected into a world of make-believe. The problem then is one of total unreality rather than that of a distance between the idealized image of the other and one's true self. On the other hand, having idealized the other, one may not only not idealize oneself, but in fact grow very unhappy with himself, increasingly fearful of the distance between the idealized one and himself. Partial idealization only accentuates the sense of his own unworthiness and unlovableness by contrast.

In either case the idealization and the fragile relationship built upon it must come to a crisis. Reality will intrude itself sometime sooner or later. The relationship will then either not survive at all, or it will start all over on a realistic and genuine course. But until that crisis comes, there will be continuous attempts to sustain the idealized situation by means of every possible expedient.

To keep from putting undue strain upon the relation, all discussion is avoided that might reveal differences.

Differences will not be faced up to at all. Jealousy, expressed or repressed, becomes a painful element in the whole affair. The jealous one fears that the other is jealous. Doubts as to the security of the relation will be further repressed. Exaggerated pretenses of mutual interest will develop more and more, and with it all there will be unending ingenuity to create responses calculated to impress and deceive the other. A certain realization of the artificiality of it all will bring pain and unhappiness, but it will inwardly be blamed upon the other, not upon oneself. A crisis is surely impending!

The final stage finds the two increasingly keeping their affair on the basis of being alone together as much as possible, avoiding broad social engagements where it would be difficult to sustain their emotinal unity, the only thing that remains intact. Even recreational fun is avoided.

As it has been pointed out by many, in the attempt to sustain such an unstable affair and the moods conducive to a romantic atmosphere, a fellow will create a "line." This "line" is subtle and somewhat effective. It keeps the romantic thought process ever present and vivid, but only by inhibiting what might otherwise be stimulating conversation.

Now surely with all of these artificial props a crisis must erupt! Genuine feelings have long been repressed. Differences have not been faced frankly and realistically, but instead the attitude has been taken that "our love will solve all problems." Dreams for the future have not been limited to what is attainable in the foreseeable future. Normal duties in daily life have not received proper attention, for the two involved have only been really concerned with "how our love is getting along." Problems have been either disregarded or glossed over, infatuation seemingly immunizing them from real concerns. There has been no stopping to count the cost of real love, and idealization has reached fantastic heights. There can only be one end and that will come through crisis. The castle must tumble!

In sharp contrast with these characteristics of romantic infatuation, loving behavior is seen to be spontaneous and natural, transparent and unaffected. It is refreshingly uncomplicated! Each person is emotionally free to be himself and to express himself. The more a person can express his real self freely, the more he can love and the more he can be loved. But infatuation made all of this impossible with its complicated emotional involvement. What may continue in a blaze of ecstasy for awhile will at last burn itself out, and then it will be seen that the flame of love, which seemed at first eternal, has grown so small as no longer to be able to keep two hearts fused together; once again they beat in their own separate time.

While love may change and the reasons for such change are more or less apparent, infatuation is subject to sudden and unpredictable turns, change that has no apparent reason at all. We have seen some of the factors which bring this about, factors inherent in the nature of infatuation which account for swift alterations of mood and behavior. Infatuation must ever be turbulent, fragile, and uncertain. It must always lead to disillusionment and frustration. How easy it is for an infatuation to turn to bitter hostility! When the relationship is undergoing stress and strain, one may suddenly take the attitude: "If that's the way he feels, well all right! I'll show him! Just watch, I'll . . . ." The tendency is frequently observed to end the relationship by breaking off quite ruthlessly, with little if any genuine concern for the feelings of the other. One turns to hate and contempt as quickly and as ardently as he was previously attracted. These feelings are often really toward himself as the result of realizing how foolishly he over-evaluated the other person. Out of pride he directs those feelings toward the other to save his own self-respect.

Even when there is no build-up to a crisis, an infatuation tends to break down rapidly. It is difficult to live in the unreal world that has been created, and difficult to find a succession of romantic situations that sustain the imagined concepts. And it is difficult to live up to the imagined conception of the other, and to the expectations that result. A person will be forced in time to realize that the object of the infatuation does not and cannot meet the imagined conception, that he loses his temper, is moody at times, is obstinate, is not always immaculately clothed. Better acquaintance will break down the extreme idealization, and one will begin to realize to what extent the other can or cannot fill the many needs of personality—that is, whether he is more than a good athlete, but is also one who can give encouragement or sympathy when needed, or be a loyal partner in some work project. In other words, when a relationship that began with infatuation continues, it goes through a change in character; it matures.

(8) Lastly, we come to the place physical attraction plays in infatuation and love. This will receive little space here as it is developed rather fully in the chapter on petting. Physical attraction plays a strong part in both infatuation and love, yet a fundamental distinction can be made. In infatuation it plays a relatively more important role in the total relationship of the two persons, whereas in love it plays a relatively less important role in the total relationship. The essential difference is based on the fact that with two persons who are in love, any physical contact tends to convey meaning, expressing what they feel toward each other in affection and mutual commitment. Moreover, self-discipline increases with consecration to the needs and larger potentials of the beloved. Everything is planned with a view toward

ensuring the happiness and welfare of the loved one. Even the sexual takes its proper place within such overall planning.

To those who are infatuated, physical contact is a pleasurable end in itself, devoid of any real meaning. It is usually camouflaged under the guise of intense romantic feelings. But a person will quite readily profess romantic affection when motivated by a strong sexual urge. Young people will sometimes deceive themselves by rationalizing a love relationship when what they really want is sexual expression only. Love is patient preparation for marriage; infatuation is haste to mate. A couple in love will look upon a necessary postponement of marriage as a period of opportunity for further preparation, so that when their marriage takes place it will be on a sounder basis than if they had married sooner. Of course there will be disappointment, but they will adjust to the necessity as one that can serve a good purpose. Quite differently is postponement of marriage received by an infatuated couple. They feel a strong urge toward immediate marriage, and consequently look upon any delay as intolerable, and as deprivation rather than preparation. They really are not sure of themselves as is the couple in love who have weathered many emotional climates, and who know how each other will act and react in many given circumstances. They can afford to wait without any sense of jeopardy to their marriage.

Infatuation can operate in one way when physical attraction is dominant, in another way when idealization is dominant. And when both are present in an infatuation, they will work at cross purposes, creating a conflict within the infatuation.

In the one case, when physical attraction dominates, the attraction will be the greater when the couple is together, and less when they are separated and physical responses are less intense and they see each other from a more realistic perspective.

In the other case, when idealization dominates, there will be greater attraction when the two are separated and the idealized image is vivid, less when they are together and they see each other as they really are and hence are more objective and critical.

The infatuated couple dare not ask such questions as: "Will he be just as happy with me when I'm not all dressed up and made up? when we must be preoccupied mostly with budget, building, and baby?" Such realistic questions as these will have been long since overshadowed by their emotional bondage to each other, and their hunger for physical contact.

A subsidiary role is given to the accommodation of life goals which the woman and the man individually have built into their separate personalities in the course of their individual experience from birth to adulthood. These may be repressed during an infatuation, but they will reassert themselves when the romantic illusion evaporates. If they ignore these basic differences, the crisis will surely come and it will shatter even the emotional unity that has been built up so strongly. Marriage would become a threat to the individual's trend of personality development.

Romance doesn't teach either the woman or the man anything about the roles they will have to play in married life. The wife-to-be will want more assurance than the old sentiment, "The hand that rocks the cradle rules the world." She will probably feel this way: "So what! I just want to know if your job will ensure our getting our own place, and let me have some help in the home, and opportunity to get out once in awhile."

The husband-to-be will not learn much about his role from romance either. It isn't sufficient simply to say that "our love will solve all problems." Romantic love and infatuation may be sure that it is strong enough to sweep away such prosaic things as money, social status, cultural dissimilarities, and parental objections. But true love will count the cost and make proper preparation for life as it is.

While it may seem like heresy to point out such difficulties as would shake the faith of those who delight in the great American fairy story, we have considered enough in these pages to realize that infatuation, or as Francis E. Merrill calls it, "a pleasant form of mass delusion," is made of the stuff of dreams. Romance is not life's greatest gift after all. Infatuation can only emphasize external characteristics that can be appreciated at once, as physical beauty and charm, youth, or vitality and vivaciousness. But love is made of sturdier stuff, and is really solid and stable.

Infatuation is a strong and subtle force that can adapt itself to varying situations and people. Fortunately, it is not so little understood as it once was. For the young person privileged to study the nature of infatuation, and who can rationally evaluate the place of romantic love, the question remains whether that one will yet succumb to the strong enticements, or will decide to wait for the development of a true love. For a Christian young person this must be made an honest matter of continual prayer.

> True love's the gift which God has given
> To man alone beneath the heaven.
> It is not fantasy's hot fire
> Whose wishes, soon as granted, fly.
> It liveth not in fierce desire;
> With dead desire, it doth not die!
> —Sir Walter Scott

7. DATES: WISE AND OTHERWISE

JUDSON and Mary Landis start us off with a definition: "Broadly speaking, the courtship period includes the entire time during which a young person is going through the process of shifting his center of affection from his own parents and family to a member of the other sex in another family. The process begins with the first date and ends with marriage." So dating is definitely the first step in the direction of marriage.

Purposeful dating is a "must" in the healthy social development of young people. With this in view, let us lay down some guiding lines. Dating contributes to three of the most crucial adjustments of human life: socialization, personality development, and selection of a mate. The social maturing will be brought about by (1) the growth in one's ability to communicate, (2) the growth of new social and cultural interests, and (3) the growth of one's personal attractiveness. So you see dating is vitally important!

The broad associations which young persons need come about through casual, diversified dating. They learn to discriminate traits in others and in themselves which cause personal likes and dislikes. Dating is the opportunity for testing social skills, and for learning how to participate confidently in groups made up of both sexes. It is a big part of maturing from adolescence into adulthood.

Dating is part of the process of being weaned emotionally from parental attachment. The adolescent transfers his emotional dependence from his parents to his contemporaries. As he finds increasing emotional satisfaction in his dates, he correspondingly finds a decreasing need for his parents. Dating helps accomplish this end through the sharing of one's interests with another, expressing one's personality before another. So dating is designed to further the process of emotional maturation.

As a new life-experience, dating may be postponed through fear of one's inadequacy. Thoughts of incompetency and embarrassment fade with experience, especially with the discovery that all young people have the same insecurities and concerns. All are in the same boat. So dating is preparation for life as it must be lived with others in the intimate mutual phases of marriage. Dating brings into being the mutual thinking and doing, working and playing of two persons, thus contributing to a full and rich life.

Young people who are dating come to appreciate the differences in masculine and feminine points of view. The strange mixture of such qualities as fickleness and unreasonableness along with other qualities such as beauty and vivacity brings a certain disillusionment, but one learns better how to cope with personality inadequacies. One is relieved from the sense of his own inadequacy. Dating helps to keep reality in perspective! The ideal person one would like to marry is measured against real persons in one's dating experience. So dating helps one properly shape the ideal image of the future spouse.

Casual, diversified dating can be a very wholesome pursuit, providing a wealth of experience in interpersonal relations. Dating affords a foretaste of the dynamics of marriage insofar as it provides opportunity for giving and taking, making decisions and solving problems though compromise of opinions and the erection of mutually acceptable purposes. Dating is the beginning of learning to adapt one's behavior to the ways and expectations of another, and to adapt because of the value of mutuality and affection.

Through dating one learns that wishing and dreaming are not enough, nor is just drifting together. Successful dating is planned and purposeful. The most wholesome and productive dates are those which develop personal knowledge, social skills, and genuine friendship. And this is best realized in those dates where the couple are participants in some activity, not merely spectators. Such dates will vary greatly, of course, from purely recreational events to work projects or serious discussions.

Dating is complex and may be variously motivated. Some date just for the fun of it, others because "everybody's doing it." Some date because it means access to social functions otherwise closed to stags. Still there are those who enjoy the competition and prestige attached to successful dating. For them it is a means of gaining social poise and improving themselves. To most daters comradeship is essential, while for many companionship in dating frankly is a part of the quest for a mate. Christensen's studies among Purdue University students show a high premium placed upon companionship, with stress on the qualities which make for easy and stimulating communication.

It would seem that the dominant pattern is for casual, diversified dating, leading on to steady, exclusive dating, and in turn to courtship. Strikingly, this is not always the case. Investigators point to the growing trend among high-school daters to go steady, whereas in college many of the same individuals will turn to casual, diversified dating. Not infrequently, courtship begins directly from this later stage of random dating.

It seems that high-school daters require emotional security and confidence in their social status. These needs are met through steady dating. By the time some of these same young persons are in college they have developed emotional maturity and social confidence to the place where they are less anxious for the emotional involvement they know to be part of going steady. Studies and vocational planning must take precedence; involvement is no longer the only dominant interest in their lives. So sometimes the process from casual to steady dating, from diversified to exclusive dating, reverses itself. Usually, however, this is not the case. Many young people do not begin their dating at all until somewhere in their college career.

Deficit dating can begin with poor health. Moodiness and lack of alertness may reflect poor habits of getting one's required rest at night. In this connection it is generally true that the quality of a date diminishes as the evening grows late, when both body and mind grow tired and dull. Fresh air, sunshine, and proper sleep are all-important elements in successful dating. The rules of hygiene and good health are directly related to dating success.

A girl, whether classically styled or not, can have charm, poise, and alertness. She can offer a lot in terms of shared interests, and an all-around keenness to the vital social concerns. One need not be a beauty queen to point for the top fellows. But one does have to be alive and creative. Vivacity belongs to the personality and spirit, and is something most girls can develop if they really want to. Natural vivacity is a quality quite different from sophistication, and is attractive where sheer beauty and sophistication may fail to be.

Christian college people are preparing for a vocation which they believe to be the will of God for their lives. They are also preparing during these days for a personal life they want to be ordered by Him. And the most crucial decision in this personal life will concern the person who becomes their married partner. Intensive study will require the devotion of many hours if one is to achieve the vocational goal. Likewise, extensive dating will require time if the personal goal is to be achieved. Good stewardship of time demands that study must not get all the best hours during these dating years. Christian fellowship, recreation, personality development in social life, and dating must all be given rightful place in one's schedule. The opportunities of these years will never return. No young person can afford to be so exclusively concerned with how to make a living as to fail to learn how to live! And learning to love is a big part of learning to live!

Studies show the educational system to be by far the most common place where young people of middle and upper-middle class meet and date. They also show that a young woman who does not begin courtship during college days has a greatly diminished prospect of marriage. While studies have not been made with reference to Christian fellowship groups, it is the author's opinion that this is by far the most important association for those involved. It is to be expected that Christian young people will find their wives and husbands in these groups. They are drawn together in such groups by the highest interests in their lives, the spiritual and moral. But this is not all. The social aspects of these Christian fellowship groups play a vital role. So also does the group advisor and the pastor of the church. Mate selection is not the prime objective of Christian youth groups, but let's be realistic—it certainly should be one of the objectives. Christian homes must emerge from Christian youth fellowship groups. It is a major duty of the church to provide such groups with proper advisors and facilities.

It is a rather common complaint of Christian girls

that the fellows in their Christian fellowship do not date as much as the non-Christian fellows they know. A little thought turns up several possible explanations. Perhaps the group fellowship lessens the sense of need for individual dating. The girls may actually have something fine in the group activities that bring them together. Courtship often begins quite directly from the associations developed in such groups. If more individual dating of members of the group were to diminish the social activities of the group as a whole, it might not be for the best interests of the girls.

Christian fellows sometimes feel inhibited because they do not have the same experience as many of their non-Christian friends. This may be due in part to the fact that they have self-imposed standards which rule out some of the more popular activities, such as affairs where drinking is a part. They may need encouragement from the girls, and they may need to learn what a broad variety of activities is open to them.

There are ways in which girls might appropriately take the initiative in getting to know fellows. Three or four girls can always arrange a party at one of their homes, or a picnic or beach party where they are going to get the food together and invite an equal number of fellows. Cooking a special foreign meal, or just providing a real spread can give them something to offer. It is a good turn-about to the commonplace expectation that the fellow always takes the girl out to eat. Both the girls and the fellows will enjoy and appreciate the innovation. And it is perfectly proper, providing a married person is along. A wholesome and enjoyable event of this kind can lead to follow-up dating of individuals as a fellow feels he has gotten to know one of the girls better. In an affair of this kind the fellows are not obligated to transport the girls, but quite generally they will arrange to see somebody home. This is often the start, isn't it?

Sometimes a fellow is uncertain as to how to ask for a date. One important rule is never to ask, "What are you doing tonight?" No girl should be put on the spot where she must declare what plans she may or may not have for the evening. Perhaps she has planned nothing and does not care to go out. It would be difficult to say this gracefully. A better approach is to ask, "I have thought it would be nice to do such and such tonight. I would love to have you go with me if you are free to do so. I'm sure we would be back by such-and-such a time." It is only fair for the fellow to state what he has in mind and when he expects to close the date. Dates should be planned, and the girl always consulted in advance. As the fellow states his plan, the girl has a moment to think whether this is attractive to her. She can decline gracefully if she wishes. Neither is embarrassed. The fellow can always say, "Oh, I'm disappointed! Perhaps another time." If the girl is not sure she would like to date the fellow, her reply might be, "I'm sorry too." If she would like to date him but isn't free that evening, her reply might be, "I'm disappointed too. I would love to go some other time."

If a girl is asked, "What are you doing tonight?" she might reply, "I'm not fully decided. What do you have in mind?" A girl has every right to ask, since she must not only decide whether this date is attractive to her, but also what must be worn to such an affair. To ask for or to accept an unplanned date may create tension and frustration unnecessarily. Uncertainty is increased for two already uncertain persons.

On first dates there tends to be lack of spontaneity and rapport. Each is intent upon impressing the other by acting out as precisely as possible the traditional etiquette he or she has learned but is somewhat uncertain of. Only as experience in dating is acquired, and as one gets to know the date better, will one feel free to act more himself. The atmosphere becomes more informal and there is more spontaneous expression of their real personalities.

Let's face the facts. Young people differ greatly in background and temperament when it comes to formal etiquette. It is easy for them to get the wrong idea on the first date if role expectations are divergent so far as etiquette is concerned. A couple who had an awkward time on their first date said later, "We just don't go for all that old folderol about the guy running around the car to open the door. We prefer to treat each other as equals and not worry about those things. We like it much better this way." Others would be ill at ease with someone who did not seem to know the courtesies. In the America of today there is no single mold. Role expectations must be discovered, and dating enhances this facility.

For two persons on their first date to establish rapport, knowing little or nothing about each other, can be no small problem. Fear or failure inhibits many from dating at all. Fear of embarrassment should the conversation lag is a common source of tension. But a few suggested steps to alleviate this fear may help.

A few thought-categories will usually serve for a whole evening of conversation. One should not concentrate his thoughts on the possibility of conversational failure, but upon the vital interests he genuinely thinks should be uppermost in young persons' lives. One should make it a point to select and read two or three articles on different current subjects, not trying to remember anything specifically, but seeking to be acquainted with the author's point of view. Above all one should confidently remember that just the ordinary interests of school and family, of future plans and goals, are a big reservoir of interesting materials for conversation. Conversation cannot be planned to any great extent; it will just develop spontaneously as interest points emerge.

One of the most effective rules for good conversationalists is to probe the interests of the other person. This brings satisfaction to both and shortens the time required to discover mutual points for sharing. Without suggesting a one-sided quiz program, we would say that the use of questions is a superior approach, providing one does not ask embarrassing personal questions. Questions about family, school, future plans, hobbies and special interests, vacation and leisure-time ideals, places visited that hold special charm—these are all worthy. Everyone needs to develop the art of asking good questions and of being a good listener. One can discover points in the replies to his questions where he may draw parallels from his own life, occasionally commenting on and enlarging the subject. Knowledge of each other is being shared, and there is the mutual satisfaction of giving and gaining, furthering the acquaintance and finding subjects for more extended discussion. When a wide range of subjects is brought into conversation, surely something will emerge that the other will latch onto and carry along. A person must only be careful not to evaluate critically what the other discloses, or to give only the information which is calculated to impress the other with one's abilities and achievements. Egocentric conversation is the most boring of all!

As friendship progresses, mutual interests will emerge and a state of rapport will be established. Both will be more at ease in the growing assurance that there are definite areas of interest which they share solidly. Small talk will more and more fill in the conversational cracks. The more ponderous subjects will be shunted onto sidetracks, held in reserve. But even in the small talk one must be careful not to choose the easy prop of derogatory remarks about people, or make dogmatic assertions on controversial subjects as though to impress the other with superior knowledge and insights. This only exhibits immaturity and causes the other to withdraw.

Sophistication is a poor way to win friendship or further dates. Affectation of worldly wisdom is unnatural and forced, and consistently creates distance between people. It smacks of aloofness and superiority, even though it may be merely the veneer of an insecure personality, the compensating attempts to cover a feeling of social inadequacy. Not all who seem sophisticated are sophisticated!

It is good to learn early in life that the natural, spontaneous expression of one's real personality is always superior. People who can be themselves, who do not take their sophistication too seriously, are usually the warm, attractive personalities liked by everyone. They're the most fun on dates you can be sure.

It is difficult to communicate with a sophisticated or affected person. A Christian young person who finds himself stuck for the evening with such an individual has a challenging task. He should be a good sport, of course, and seek to make the date constructive. A good-humored attempt to break down the sophistication is not out of order, just so it isn't obvious. Perhaps the other really longs for some help so he or she may know the joy of simply being onself. Friendly chatter about little things will sometimes turn the trick. Do not stand in awe of the seemingly sophisticated person; recognize rather that it is most probably the cover for a personality need. You may be the very one whose spontaneous expression of personality can help meet that need.

It is easy to let the other person know you like him or her by just being yourself and showing that you are having a good time. Sophistication or aloofness, on the other hand, will convey the idea that the date was not enjoyed. And decidedly one does not have to become possessive to show affection or to give security to the association. A possessive attitude is perhaps one of the chief single hindrances to further dates.

As to the hour a date should close, this is perfectly proper for the girl to suggest if her date has not already done so. Fellows are often uncertain about this and would appreciate knowing the girl's desire. They do not want to spoil the date by taking the girl home before her evening is complete, nor make the mistake of creating undue anxiety by keeping her out later than she had planned, or by letting her fear that this might happen. It is better to have this understood. The fellow may suggest a time and ask if this fits in with her expectations. If he fails to do this, the girl may say early in the evening "My parents and I have agreed on a 10:30 deadline for a week-night date, so we can enjoy ourselves until then before we call it a day." Or a girl on campus can mention the house rule and her desire to cooperate so as not to hinder the possibility of further dates.

Since dating is the beginning of the process that carries through to mate selection and to marriage, the quality of dates ought to reflect that end-object. Dating which precedes exclusive courtship can major on the requisites to good companionship. To simply have this in mind will suffice for eliminating much that is superficial in the typical dating pattern.

Strange, but some of life's highest values come to us not because we strive for them, but come while we play! Playing is an important phase of living. Recreation is a prime medium for personal growth. All work and no play, you know, makes Jack a dull boy. It robs Jack of enriching experiences. And all play of the same kind can make a dull person too. A variety of skills and interests to fill leisure hours is the most desirable. Isn't it true that a couple exhibit limited mental and social resources when they always have to go some place and purchase entertainment? They should be able to create many of their good times out of their own resources.

Group dating is an excellent thing. Those who are intent upon meeting that one-and-only frequently fail to understand the powerful influence of group dating in this connection. Whether an individual's dating begins early in high school or halfway through college, group dating is the natural approach to successful individual dating. In group dating one finds it is easier to talk to the other sex than was thought. One learns to regard members of the other sex as interesting persons, and friendships follow. One discovers that the sexes have more in common than differentiate them. One also feels more at ease because there are others present to hold up the conversation and to broaden the range of subjects. Attention is spread around a little more, and daters are kept from too much emotional intensity. Such experience is good insurance against the immature reactions of possessiveness, envy, and jealousy which frequently express themselves in individual dating.

In group dating one develops an ability to discern personality types, to learn why some persons are attractive and others are not. Testing his own social skills, one observes what others like or do not like about him. From first being able to notice the gross differences in persons, one increasingly learns to discern the more subtle shades of personality difference in dating partners. Personal traits stand out in groups that are sometimes hidden in individual dating. For instance, one may become a loud show-off, or monopolize the conversation, or act sullen and moody when he cannot dominate the group. Better to see these traits expressed in a group than gradually to realize they exist after becoming involved with such a person.

Group dating is the only advisable occasion for Christians to have any dating relationship with non-Christians, or with those who are racially or socially from much different backgrounds. This is the only acceptable way to accept a "blind" date, and here we refer to a blind date only in the sense that it is a date with someone unknown to oneself, but well known to the friend who arranged it.

Group activities bring out and round out personality. If there are games, one learns to live by the rules and abide by the decisions. It is vital to learn how to take defeat and be a good loser. One cannot be a good sport, or maintain a close relationship with another person, and always have his own way. Dating provides experience in compromising for the sake of the mutual good of both persons. Such qualities as honesty, cooperativeness, and responsibility come to the surface in group activities. In the same circumstances one can compare the reactions of the dating partner with those of others.

Such activities as sports, excursions, beach suppers and the like are always more fun when others are along to share the fun. Furthermore, a dull dating partner will not spoil the fun when others are included. What a close and enriching human experience can come from intimate small groups! To cook and eat together, to play together, or to discuss the great issues of life together in the natural surroundings of God's great out-ot-doors, and in the company of intimate friends, is a deepening experience. And one of the real tests of successful marriage is the ability of two persons to meet new people and assimilate them into their friendships, to adapt to new situations, and to enjoy a satisfying social life with others. This should be discovered during dating days.

Christian young people are restricted in some areas of social life because of self-imposed standards of right conduct. This suggests the need for a variety of social substitutes. Still there are available sources of activity which serve as substitutes for that which is less desirable. For example a hobby club, such as a camera club, is a splendid idea. The two can take it up together. Or a world of good times can be had in attending an evening school course during the winter. Creative outlets bring high personal satisfaction, and at the same time provide opportunity for getting to know much about another person. It's a good idea to vary the nature of such interests so as not to get into the narrow rut of one specialty only. You may discover that purposefully changing courses will introduce both persons to absorbing fields of interest never dreamed of before.

Entertaining at home should not be overlooked. The possibilities are great. Your home is a place where your friends ought to see and know you. Let your friends meet your parents in this way, and let your parents meet your friends. It's not likely your parents will settle down for the evening with your friends. They are not likely to spoil the fun this way. And if you really fear they might, just talk to your parents before the evening, discuss your plans for the evening, and settle upon the time and length of their appearance. Your friends will appreicate the intimacy of such a get-together, recognizing the personal effort expended for their entertainment.

As for what to do at a home get-together, remember that home is characterized by warm informality, and activities should be in keeping. Home is home; it is not a place of commercial entertainment. So charades might be fun, or a time of listening to good music, or a game or two, or just a discussion of some vital subject. An exciting evening can be built around a home-cooked foreign-style meal with rather elaborate decorations which carry through the motif. Remember the other values of home entertainment discussed earlier.

Dates in which young people can express their lives

in Christian service have unusual value. Sharing a common service motive, planning and presenting a spiritual program to others, meeting needs other than their own, and being concerned with something besides how their date is getting along, is all wholesome experience in successful dating. Christian personality can grow, and two persons can discover something meaningful about each other in the most important area of life, that of outgoing love and service for others.

This kind of service project is best arranged as part of the Christian youth fellowship program. Is this not a strong reason why young people ought ot keep a close relationship with their fellowship group, doing their part to make it a vital fellowship and service organization? The compensations of this kind of pursuit will prove far superior to those of dating which offers little more than two persons living emotionally upon the personality of each other.

Dating ought never to deteriorate into a socal grab-bag. Competitive dating is too often thoughtless and cruel. It is usually a sure way for a Christian to lose the respect which he desires for his testimony's sake. Exploitative dating is always wrong. It must be more than a way to gain as many self-enhancing attachments as possible. It is all too easy to do this under the guise of gaining broad acquaintances. One must be honest before God in searching his motives for dating.

Social stratification prevails in our culture, but should have a diminishing significance to the growing Christian. Campus codes which "rate the date" should be replaced by a more realistic and sound system of evaluating dates. Too commonly the measure is based on aspects of popularity. This whole concept voids the possibility of dating as a means of getting to know people of varied types, gifts, and backgrounds. Within the current pattern, a fellow too often feels it is imperative that he date a girl with extensive dating experience, who is accomplished in the arts of getting along in a crowd in a charming manner. The dater wants assurance of such success in his date. He is motivated by ego-enhancement, and bows to a system that rates dates in a superficial way.

Christian groups afford the best solutions for breaking down the caste system set up on some campuses by the "ins" to exclude the "outs." This status concept is derived directly from the social caste system set up by adults in their own communities.

Not only are the "ins" snobbish, but the "outs" become snobbish too. They are consciously rejected and want to be in position to reject others, so they in turn reject both the "ins" and other "outs." They tend to withdraw and isolate themselves, justifying their behavior on such premises as that "Studies must come first," or "Who cares about dating anyway?"

This caste system with its superficial rating techniques can be eclipsed if not abolished by the democracy of Christian fellowship groups. These fellowship groups ought to be the chief means of accomplishing group dating, providing the mutual friendships that so often lead directly to serious, exclusive dating and on to courtship.

Christian young people who feel themselves excluded from certain popular campus activities should not withdraw and seclude themselves! To be subject to wounded pride with its bitter resentments and withdrawal is just as immature as the system that provokes it. Better to give oneself to the work of being part of the planning committee for the social events within a vital Christian youth group. Better to be part of the answer than part of the problem! In the long run this experience will prove the richest and most rewarding of all. That's a guarantee!

I am afraid few fellows have ever thought of the Christian ministry of dating. Let me explain how this operates.

Christian personality should be growing and influential during dating days. This means that dating need not be selfish anymore than it need be exclusive at first. Since much dating is really pride-motivated, with fellows dating only when the most desirable girls are available, there can be real joy for the Christian fellow who will date the girl less popular and so far passed by. Some real surprises of a truly gratifying nature may be in store. He may accomplish something very worthwhile, not only for the girl but for himself. If he is a fine Christian person, none will think the less of him. In fact, someone more desirable may take note and gain an interest in him because of this very quality observed in his dating tactics. The less popular girl may be the contact for meeting another who will have higher appeal, the one date leading directly to another with this more attractive person. Or the less popular girl may prove to be an outstanding person, to be appreciated for what she is in herself, not for the way she measures up to a superficial standard. At any rate, the two will have grown in worthwhile experience, and surely God will honor such dating conduct.

There is another traditional approach that Christian young people might re-think. Three out of four men state that they prefer their wife to be younger, desiring on the average a difference of about two years. Four out of five women polled state that they would like their husband to be older by about three years. In actuality, wives on the average are a little less than three years younger than their husbands. The man's ego and the wife's desire for greater security are undoubtedly major factors in this culturalized preference. The practical consequence is that since on the average the woman lives five years longer than the man, she will spend eight years in widowhood.

At the heart of the Christian marriage concept lies the ideas of equality and mutuality. The achievement of oneness in Christian marriage does not require an age difference. From the author's observations it would seem the better thing for young men to date those in the same class at school, or the same fellowship group at church. It would tend to reduce the exploitative possibilities on the one hand, and give maximum dating security to the girls in the group on the other. Christian fellowship groups would have a greater stability as dating was more and more confined within it.

The theme of this chapter is dates, wise and otherwise. Some thoughts have been presented along the line of wise dating. The remainder will deal with two major problem areas in the dating structure.

First, interracial dating is a trouble spot. Interracial dates should not be accepted unless one is prepared to consider interracial marriage. And while neither anthropological nor Biblical reasons stand against such marriage, there are weighty sociological considerations which cannot be ignored.

In countries such as Brazil or Hawaii where race mixture involves no social stigma, the result is the blending of two cultures; prejudice and segregation present no problem. But where racial pride and the conviction of superiority are strong on the part of one race, such as in the United States, racial amalgamation fosters extreme bitterness and social strife. In our country the long history of superiority feeling on the part of the whites follows the early subjection of the Negro to slavery and his subsequent degradation. Culturally we have kept the Negro degraded for the most part, there being some notable exceptions of course. One consequence is reflected in the laws of twenty-nine states against the marriage of Negroes and whites. The problem is compounded by the number of illegitimate children coming from such unions.

Christianity has a crusading idealism that always goes cross-current to the world's social standards. Yet Christians cannot afford to ignore society as it exists at any given time, nor can they ignore the right principles required to bring about change. Despite the dreams and attempts of idealists, the history of change in the societal patterns is for the most part that of gradual change. Sociologists point out that there must be a continuity of culture and tradition or there is social disaster. Rapid transitions are freighted with potential dangers. Needless suffering and chaos are brought about by those who insist on immediate change without counting the cost or planning a good strategy.

While there has been a gradually developing culture of intermarriage in Hawaii where the fewer problems have undergone better assimilation, there is even a cultural problem there that serves as an illustration. Intermarriage between Chinese and Japanese is relatively low, and the divorce rate decidedly high. This contrasts with the successful intermarriage of both Chinese and Japanese with Hawaiians and others. This failure is attributed to the fact that both Chinese and Japanese have complete and strongly differentiated cultures.

This provides something of a key to the problem in our country. The biggest barrier is not color, but the culture which the color represents. In the minds of the majority this is too great a barrier to hurdle.

Interracial marriage where there is a radical color difference creates serious problems for any children that come. Not infrequently there is a very dark child and a very light one in the same family. The colored child loves the colored parent and dislikes the other. Or the parent takes to the child of the same color but rejects the other. Or the children themselves dislike each other. This is aggravated when other children make fun of the fact that two children in the same family are different in color. Our cruel and competitive culture still brands such children as "half-breeds." So the crucial question is whether parents have a right to impose upon unborn generations a radical decision of their own.

Every research scale of marriage predictability makes it clear that the wider the cultural differences the less chance there is for marriage success. Granted, many obstacles are hurdled by two persons who are one in their mutual faith in and love for Jesus Christ. But two persons must never assume that spiritual identity will necessarily overcome every and all obstacles. Background, status, custom and family rituals all enter as potent factors in marital adjustment. A dependent parent living in the young couple's home might accentuate the cultural difference to the breaking point. All of this must be considered.

The fact that racial prejudice is a wicked and abhorrent thing does not alter the fact that it exists and influences social adjustment in the community. The mounting problems of personal insecurity in child life are grave enough without adding the possibility that children of interracial marriages will find themselves regarded as "outsiders" by the majority of youngsters. Overwhelming inferiority will make them curse the parents whose selfish love forced this unwanted life upon them.

It is sheer idealism for a couple to think that their broadmindedness and example will pave the way to greater tolerance in the community. To ignore the ostracism of their non-Christian neighbors may be acceptable to them, but it is hardly acceptable to their children, their parents, their friends, or their church as it seeks to witness to a community whose confidence it must first secure. And for such a couple to seek to solve the problem by not having children is a tacit admission that the relationship is wrong. Just to mention one of the many side-problems presently associated with interracial marriage in our country: Why is the chief involvement that of colored men who want white women? This is regarded as exploitative, and hence adds to the disfavor of such marriages.

The incidence of interracial marriage in the United States seems high in view of the acute social pressures against it. This raises an interesting question: In what social classes is this found? Two groups stand out: lower economic groups where racial mixture is found residentially, and in groups of college intellectuals.

In the instance of the lower economic groups the principle of propinquity operates. Young people are brought together residentially, form neighborhood and school friendships, and marry. Unfortunately, low economic groups are usually where low social and moral standards are also to be found. So long as this is the prime source of interracial marriage in the United States, prejudice against such marriages will prevail.

Strikingly, the incidence of interracial marriage is high among college intellectuals. The reasons are apparent. Young persons of different racial backgrounds are sometimes drawn together in societies where the requirement is intellectual. Academic achievements are not limited to any race, and such achievements will draw young people together. Another factor is the novelty of different backgrounds and the fascination which fires the imagination of venturesome youth. For others such alliances begin as protest moves against prevailing patterns in the national culture. Some persons seem to thrive on the unconventional. They are self-appointed reformers, idealists who think the best approach to social reform is to personally defy convention, public opinion, and present structures. They would take things into their own hands, following an individual solution with little attempt to be part of a larger, thought-through approach. Sometimes the protest is against parental domination, knowing that interracial dating or interracial marriage will hurt the parents. It is not un-qualified love for the other person that leads to mar-riage, but resentment against the parents. And lastly, an unpopular girl in her own group may succumb to the at-tentions of an attractive and perhaps well-to-do young man of another race.

Once in a while a carefully thought-through and prayed-through relationship of this kind comes into being and is successful. Usually there is something to show its rightness in a particular instance, such as a call to Christian service in an area where the marriage will be accepted. Since this is the rare exception, however, young people should resist the temptation to use this as justification for an involvement.

This whole matter is a decision to be made when one is contemplating his standards for dating, not after an involvement has happened and become emotionally powerful. The person weighing interracial dating should remember three things by way of principle: (1) the problem of interracial marriage is relative to the degree of difference between the two cultures involved, (2) it is relative to the degree of social approval or disapprov-al (including that of the families involved), and (3) since these factors are more significant to marriage than to dating, dates may not sufficiently impress one with the serious problems ahead.

The second problem area relates to interfaith mar-riages. Suffice it to touch upon the heart of the matter for a Christian young person.

One's relationship to Christ is a whole way of life, not merely a matter of what church one attends and what creed one holds. These are basic, of course, but the problem is broader. There are established forms of worship which distinguish different Protestant churches. There are widely differing theological points of view. There are cultural configurations typical of individual Christian groups. Basic life-values may be highly divergent. Scruples as to social issues are by no means consistent among Protestant groups. Such questions as the role of religious education in the family, financial support of religious causes, participation in activities which involve the whole family—all of these are crucial to marital adjustment, increasing in prominence as the family develops. There are even national aspects. One only need think of Scotch Presbyterians, German Lutherans, English Methodists, Dutch Reformed, and one can realize that there are cultural patterns typical of some churches.

One may be surprised to find social stratification among Protestant churches, but it is there. So it is wisest to make sure that one's denominational background is similar to that of one's dating companion if there is to be more than one date in view. It should not need to be said that a young person who truly knows and loves the Lord Jesus Christ must resist every temptation to date seriously a person who does not share this same faith and love.

Purposeful dating is a "must" in the well-rounded life of an earnest Christian young person. Dating should be a vital part of one's prayer interest. It is a chief area which requires the blessing and direction of God. And young people who turn to Him can be sure that data for dating is still part of God's business!

8. PROFILE ON PETTING

THE very essence of the petting question is whether one's association with a person of the other sex shall be based chiefly on the physical or the social plane, and whether it is purely a pleasurable pastime, or the symbol of a permanent oneness in love. This very question reveals at once how intricate the problem really is, and why it is apparently difficult for a majority of young people to understand and evaluate the implications for themselves. Some frankly put their association chiefly on the physical plane, others on the social. But for many the distinction is not clear enough, and the relationship becomes something of both. When one's values are confused it is easy to fall into inferior ways of conduct.

Petting has an indefinable quality about it, since an individual reacts as a whole, not as a series of disconnected anatomical parts. Nor can the physical be separated from the psychological. Petting has physiological, psychological and social effects and implications. It has also spiritual implications which make it sacramental. One's behavior, then, can only be evaluated in terms of what happens to him as a person, not merely in terms of what part of his anatomy is involved in what particular process. So "necking" and "petting" belong to the overall process of personal interaction.

This is not to say, however, that there is not a very real boundary separating the lightly exhilarating touch of affection from the more highly stimulating touch we term petting. While it is largely variation in degree, petting is sexual stimulation that leads directly to loss of personal control, to sinful thoughts and acts. The problem is to determine where the boundary is to be located in a Christian young person's conduct. The point where personal integrity is violated, where inhibitions are broken down to the place where one's idealism has been compromised, is the point we must discover.

Personality is so constituted by God that there is a deep and abiding sense of personal dignity. To the enlightened Christian there is a sacredness about one's body and its functions. Chastity involves not only the acts but the thoughts of a person as they relate to the body, either one's own or another's. Chastity rests upon the acknowledgement of the sanctity of sex. Chastity, as Norman Pittenger points out, is sexual life according to the ordering of God's plan and purpose. A chaste person is one whose sexual life in all of its facets is rightly instrumental in the fulfillment of the divine purpose. It is a positive rather than a negative concept. When sex is instrumental in expressing a love which is given by God, it is chaste. When it is instrumental in expressing an end in itself, it is not chaste. It is perversion in purpose, more so than in act, that brings unchastity into being. Control is an inferior goal, a negative approach; chastity is a positive goal, serving positive purposes. A chaste person is not as interested in margins of safety as in true purposes. Discipline in matters of sex must not merely serve negative fears and standards, but rather positive, divine purposes! Sex expression has a special key to a person's soul, and that key must be used at the proper time. Sex is a sacred power and must be directed by God. One's sexual life, then, is one of those divine secrets that is to be shared at the right time, with the right person, for the right purpose. Chastity has to do altogether with divine purpose!

In every physical expression of affection there is an intuition in the human personality that something uniquely precious to one's personal dignity has been given to another. Accordingly, there is an expectation that something binding and abiding will issue from that self-giving. But it is abiding only when two persons are committed to each other in a marriage that will preserve the gift. Thus one may not give oneself in such expressions outside of marriage without experiencing a loss of self-respect.

The considerable freedom of physical contact between the sexes in our day creates a problem for young people in knowing how to discriminate between the degree of contact that is wise and beneficial, and that which is unwise, full of risk, and emotionally destructive. In this connection a girl has the delicate problem of where to draw the line in sex appeal. This is something she can govern to a certain extent. Undeniably, the desire of a person to make himself or herself attractive to members of the opposite sex is a legitimate part of mate selection, and sex appeal is one of a number of legitimate and necessary elements of attractiveness. The real question is what form the appeal should take and to what lengths it should go. The initial question of sex appeal and personal attractiveness later becomes the question of what physical contact shall be correlated with it. The answer to these questions is not in moralizing, but in intelligently coming to terms with all of the factors involved. We shall see that in the matter of petting the arguments against it are weightier than those for it. Despite the suggestions of Dr. Kinsey, a strong array of authorities support this position.

Petting is a process of physical and emotional involvement between two persons of opposite sex. It consists of kissing and fondling of a nature that tends to be sexually exciting and stimulating. It is physical contact for pleasure which is an end in itself, and involves fondling the erogenous zones, even to the point of bringing about an orgasm, but does not include sexual intercourse. In petting there is necessarily a deliberate attempt to effect sexual arousal. In marriage the same thing is called foreplay because it comes before and prepares the couple for intercourse. When petting is merely two persons enjoying themselves through each other, it is mutual lust. It is not calculated on their part to help them meet as persons at all, and something less than personality is fulfilled. With others, to be sure, especially among engaged couples, petting is a part of the seeking to meet and love as persons committed to each other. In either case, as petting is indulged outside of marriage and apart from intercourse, the deepest yearnings of personality are obscured and sidetracked by the more immediate pleasures. Habituated petting makes one more and more a slave to immediate pleasures, the kind of pleasures that come the easiest way.

Some fellows pet as a compulsive means of reassuring themselves that they can love someone, or that they themselves are lovable. Some girls pet because they think it is the necessary price for popularity, forgetting that such popularity is superficial, and more often than not will rebound against them. If a girl pets to be popular, she is probably popular only because she pets. She deceives herself into thinking that she is liked for herself and for her personal qualities, whereas in fact she is only a more or less convenient means to an end. She should ask herself why she fears she will not get dates unless she pets. Has she so few assets that she must depend only upon something so restricted as sex appeal? Better far that she should remedy the underlying cause for her lack of popularity than to depend upon something as limited as sexual attraction. Of course, if a girl realizes all this and yet chooses to continue her petting, then for her petting has become a form of rationalization, a cheap substitute for the solution to a basic problem in her personality. Petting can never make a person popular for the reason that popularity is a complex of many elements: appearance, personal charm, abilities and attitudes, moods and emotions, specific skills in a variety of things, and especially warm and open friendliness. As a matter of fact, popularity gained by petting alone is restrictive of virtually all of these other elements, and becomes a means of inhibiting personal desirability.

Romantic love at times is rationalized, so that young people who have been conditioned by the cult of romance to put their present love feelings above everything else will justify their petting.

For many girls, petting is not the price of popularity especially, but it is considered the price for an evening's entertainment. ("But he spent so much money on me I could hardly refuse his wishes!") For such a young lady there needs to be some solid thinking, for she has already commercialized the relationship in her mind. This is really the essence of harlotry.

A girl is not necessarily prudish who refuses to pet. Nor can she be accused of a puritanical touch-me-not attitude. It may be purely a matter of fastidiousness. She reserves the right to decide who may and who may not kiss and fondle her. This is a personal right to be highly respected, as all personal rights are.

This would hardly be a fair treatment of petting if it were not to trace the incitements to pet that arise out of adolescent development. We shall consider just three that are typical and common.

(1) With the new awareness of the difference between the sexes, an adolescent awakens to a strong de-

sire to have a more intimate knowledge of the other sex. This is partly curiosity and fascination, partly sexual awakening. Exploring the distinctive nature of the opposite sex becomes a means of understanding the uniqueness of one's own sex. Petting is sometimes initiated as one of the more direct ways toward gaining this knowledge. A factor in this is the awareness that one has the ability to attract an avid interest from a member of the opposite sex. It is a part of maturing and self-assurance to want to know to what extent one has this personal power to attract. For the girl it is an awareness of her sex appeal, and for the boy it is the attractive power of his masculinity. Deep within both is the craving for knowledge of self and of others in their essential being. This new dimension of sex-differentiation enhances their desire to know what new and novel ways of personal interaction are possible because of this difference, and what exciting new possibilities are hidden therein.

(2) Following this awakening there comes an awareness of the ecstatic pleasure of contact with the other sex. There is the general excitement of personal interaction with the other sex, the winning of attention, and the apparent fascination of another with oneself. While this is largely sexual, it is also psychological and social. The mutual stimulation through interaction between persons whose natures are so different meets a very real need in both male and female personality. Vaguely one becomes aware of the close connection between aesthetic pleasure and sexual stimulation, although the connection may not be understood. Music, dance rhythms, and artistic beauty all seem to blend into the process of attraction between the sexes, giving a different quality to many facets of life which were hitherto unnoticed. For the fellow this focuses quite sharply as sexual stimula-

tion, whereas for the girl it is a more general and diffused excitement.

(3) Much in line with the suggestion just presented is the adolescent need to be needed. This is another of the factors which motivates attachment with a member of the opposite sex. Early there is an awareness that the nature of the opposite sex is complementary and that each sex has something to offer the other. For many this emerges as simply the possibility of mutual pleasure. It is a strong element in attraction. Essentially it is a need for reassurance of one's desirability and lovableness, as well as reassurance of one's capability of loving and caring for another. One maintains status in his own eyes by successfully bringing another person into a mutual experience of petting and its pleasure. Sexual pleasure is thereby mingled deeply with one's need for self-assurance. It is a workable means of alleviating the emotional pain of thinking oneself unlovable and unacceptable by the other sex. From this perspective, petting can be something of a consolation prize for one's deficiencies in successful personal interaction with the other sex. Frustrated and unsuccessful in other pursuits of life, a young person may choose success in petting as an alternative. Petting may even be a way of holding a date when other ways fail.

By its very intensity of emotional attachment, petting deceives one into thinking that successful personal interaction has been achieved at last. So petting may sometimes be representative of a compulsive need for self-assurance and status, and so the mark of a dependency relation.

Unhappiness and insecurity at home may prompt a young person to find satisfaction and consolation in this kind of indulgence, the roots of his trouble being not really sexual at all, but going deeper into his failure to make a real adjustment to life. Sexual fulfillment of this type has become a way of escape, a means of feeling important through the mastery of someone else.

Once in awhile it is suggested that petting is a good thing for the maturing of young people, that it is an educative process preparing one for marriage by filling in the transitional steps from immaturity to full heterosexuality. This is a dangerous half-truth, for petting is educative to be sure, but it is education which belongs to the process within marriage itself. Science tells us that there is no such thing as sexual incompatibility; what goes under that name is usually emotional or interpersonal incompatibility that affects the sexual relation. The one who pets must realize that to dissociate sexual compatibility from the full-robed compatibility of marriage is to risk achieving any kind of real compatibility at all. To make sexual compatibility a substitute for personal compatibility is to block off the possibility of any true compatibility. It is for this reason, among others, that young people who have been physically intimate end up by breaking off their relationship altogether in many instances.

Dr. Kinsey discovered that petting to climax, that is, petting to an orgasm, is used frequently by young men in the upper social and educational brackets of our society. The reasons for this are not hard to find. Such young persons are searching for the best way to satisfy their emotional natures and at the same time preserve their moral integrity. Their behavior is determined not so much by the fear of social restriction as it is by their own inner code of what is right. That code is generally inadequate in our day because of the sex-saturation of our culture and the arbitrary or anemic declaration of Christian moral principles. So petting to a climax is evidently not seen in its true moral implications, and is indulged in order to avoid sexual intercourse itself while at the same time releasing sexual tension. Kinsey reported that 58 per cent of the men investigated in the upper educational levels pet until orgasm occurs. Kinsey, however, jumped to an unwarranted conclusion in stating that there is considerable evidence that premarital petting experience contributes definitely to the effectiveness of the sexual relationship in marriage. An array of authorities disagree with him on this.

Petting to climax is indulged by upper-level educational males for other reasons. They are older students who must postpone marriage until they finish school. For them it has the advantage of being accessible under conditions where intercourse would be impossible. Most petting is done in an automobile. Petting to climax provides a simpler means of achieving both arousal and orgasm, making such an experience possible whenever it is desired and without fear of pregnancy resulting. For the same reason college men cannot marry they cannot afford a pregnancy in another. Many state that their reason for resorting to petting to climax is that it preserves a girl's virginity. A Christian must take a second look at this reason, and ask whether it shows a true understanding of what it means to violate the integrity of another person. The reason will not hold up in the Christian view.

Kinsey also suggests that petting which does not proceed to a climax may seriously disturb a person, possibly leaving one or both individuals in a state of nervous tension, a tension that may produce hypersensitivity and an increased irritability, all of which in time will strain the relationship of the couple and possibly prevent the development of love and the desire for marriage.

This conclusion of Kinsey suggests that it is better to pet to climax, or not to pet at all. This narrows the consideration, and the Christian really must face the fact that petting to climax is morally little different from intercourse itself, yet petting but not to climax is generally considered psychologically harmful. The alternative, obviously, is to refrain from this kind of indulgence altogether.

Some will argue that petting is right when it is restricted to couples who are engaged. But here there is a serious problem. Two things must be noted: first, that one out of three engagements are broken off and do not eventuate in marriage. These are national statistics. Perhaps this would be somewhat less among Christian young people. But even the possibility that an engagement might be broken should show that petting is a mistake. Secondly, habitual petting is actually given as one of the chief causes for the breaking of engagement. So it is a dangerous thing to say that petting may be allowed because a couple is engaged. There are those, too, who would normally break an engagement because of problems that would indicate such a decision was wise, but who, because they had indulged in petting, felt they should marry anyway. In whatever way the problem is viewed, petting is not a recommended part of engagement.

Young people confront the option of petting with neither experience nor maturity to guide them. The freedom of our day has largely increased the problem. Kimball Young, the sociologist, says: "The automobile has done more to change the patterns of courtship than anything that has happened in two thousand years." The automobile provides a private boudoir, and quickly transports young people away from any possible interference by family or friends. While they may assume that being alone in an automobile creates privilege, they must rather learn to regard it as heightened responsibility, a challenging test of personal integrity and self-discipline. It precipitates emotional crises for the immature young person. Automobiles provide the kind of intimate privacy that is conducive to, and invites, love-making. When to this is added the sentimental music of the car radio, or perhaps the stimulation of an exciting outdoor movie, the urge to pet may be insistent. Even a double date can prove no help in this direction at all if the other couple is advanced in their love-making practices and their example puts demands upon the couple not out for that kind of thing.

Just being together forges strong emotional attachments between two young persons. This in turn is strengthened by every gesture of physical affection. Young people expect something abiding to remain from their expressions of affection, for they feel that such expressions are the giving of something precious to one's personal dignity. What has been given cannot be taken back, so therefore it should remain. A process develops in the attempt to keep this expectation from collapsing. To avoid the disappointment of realizing that a personal dimension did not emerge as expected, that nothing will necessarily abide from their giving, young people find themselves compulsively increasing the frequency and intensity of their petting. To some couples engaged to be married this petting experience may be regarded by them as the symbolic extension of their growing oneness. But for young people not committed to each other in this way, there can be no such significance. It is a premature expression that can only lead to much frustration and inner conflict of values. Apart from its intended consummation in intercourse, it is only an abortive experience.

Habitual petting may have the result of cheapening sex in the minds of the two, and deprive any genuine expression of its real meaning. It may come to stand for all there is in the sexual relationship of marriage, and remove the proper expectations of marriage. The couple indulging in petting may assume that sex is a burden and that apparently marriage has very little more to offer them.

Petting does not stand alone; it is the natural prelude to the intimacies of marriage. The unnatural thing is that petting should not be followed by such intimacies. To allow petting, but not its natural issue, is to plunge into emotional conflict, frustration, and into a physiological state that demands relief. Petting to climax provides that relief, but in doing so it further removes from one's understanding the full ecstasy and joy that is meant to consummate such arousal. The orgasm that results from petting is an empty, hollow experience in comparison to the consummation of intercourse within the love and commitment of marriage.

The nervous tension which frequently results from petting is cause for resentfulness when one does not understand that it is not something in the other person, but the incomplete process, that has caused the disappointment. The resentfulness that arises may easily turn into strong hostility toward the other person, and actually thwart an otherwise genuine growth of love between the two. Through fostering the very opposite of what was expected, such petting might successfully end the relationship entirely. This is not infrequently a girl's reaction to the whole thing.

The two who decided to go ahead with petting simply because they thought their relationship was for keeps then have room for genuine regret that they ever shared so deeply with another under the pretense that never came to pass. And such regrets have a strange way of living on in memory, and sometimes of affecting later behavior responses.

Petting experiences tend to become more and more vivid in the imagination. They are stored in memory as permanent residents of the subconscious. They may be repressed, but memory has a way of bringing them up at a later time. They may be brought back after marriage, construed by imagination to seem like a present unfaithful episode. How often young people have said in private conferences that these seem to be the only experiences they do retain vividly in their memories. Sinful human nature is like that. Guilt and regret remain long after to do their inhibiting and spoiling work in the lives of people who never remotely conceived the power of guilt when the mistake was made. Inhibitions emerge later in married life which ought not to arise, and they trace their origin to habituated petting before marriage. When past experiences do not return in later life as conscious awareness in the form of guilt and regret, they still may come in the form of inhibitions that cripple personality. Some of the inhibitions which develop with habitual petting carry over into marriage, bringing emotional disturbances and undue maladjustments. Perhaps it is the constant exercise of control under stress in order to prevent going too far which creates lasting inhibitions that continue on in marriage. We are only beginning to understand the extent of the disadvantage that petting can bring into marriage. Of all things it is not an innocent pastime!

It is important to understand the difference between stimulation and satisfaction. Petting is sexual stimulation, not satisfaction. Even petting to climax is classified as stimulation, for while it brings physiological release, it falls short of the personal dimension of true satisfaction. It ends in tension. And as one can see, failure to understand this will lead to false expectations.

The unintended progression usually develops when two persons are least able to evaluate it rationally or resist it emotionally. To their sadness, many a couple has found that stopping is increasingly more difficult as the stages advance. For a young person to say, "This will not go any farther next time," is to underestimate the power of the progression. How easy it is for emotional excitement and sexual stimulation to overcome both one's reason and will! To decide to go no farther in moments when there is no sexual excitement or emotional intoxication is one thing; to be able to abide by it later is quite another.

Holding hands is a form of stimulation that has its own tolerance point. That tolerance point is where diminishing returns make an urgent demand for something more. Kissing and embracing follow and in turn have their own tolerance point. Then the demand is for caressing, light at first, but leading on eventually to petting, to manipulation of the erogenous zones to excite full sexual arousal.

This progression must be guarded carefully, knowing that it is virtually impossible to return to and maintain an earlier stage of physical expression, and then only with multiplied frustrations. For then the young couple know what is beyond, and it is difficult to be satisfied at all with less than they have experienced.

Many girls like and can stand light petting better than fellows, and can be more satisfied to begin and end with caresses, absorbed in the pleasures that are diffused throughout their whole natures. The same girls may be quite ignorant of masculine reactions. They are not usually fully aware that the sex drive of a fellow has reached a peak in middle and late teens, whereas their own will not reach its greatest power until at least a decade later. Girls are generally at a disadvantage in evaluating the reactions of fellows. They are unaware of the readiness with which fellows respond to stimuli of sight and touch in a way remote from their own experience. They have no way of knowing how the sexual drive is concentrated in the male, demanding intercourse not petting. And as a result, a girl can easily permit the first steps toward petting to occur unnoticed, only to be surprised and upset later when the fellow's inclinations become more apparent. By then a fellow may be too stimulated to be easily put off. One must remember, too, that a person tends to expect and to demand the level of physical expression to which he has become accustomed through habit, not what either his or her ideal may dictate.

Petting does not build up tolerance against further desire, but only stimulates that desire the more, reducing tolerance against it. We have noted that in sexual excitement an individual's perspective and rational point of view may be easily superseded by emotion, with the result that control will be lost. One cannot be sure of his self-control under such circumstances, and it is sheer folly to think otherwise. It is illogical for a couple, neither of whom is willing to go the whole way, to pet until both are teased and tantalized almost beyond all hope of control, letting it become a contest to see how far they can go before the emotional demands become unendurable. This is to make their whole relationship as difficult as possible, rather than as easy as possible. It puts an almost impossible pressure against their standard, thought out in more rational moments. The petting once begun carries along by its own momentum, becoming a Frankenstein that its creator can no longer manage. It is certainly foolish for a couple to rationalize that they are so easily tempted to have intercourse that their best protection is to relieve the problem by petting. Actually they are advancing closer to the place where they just cannot resist temptation.

Petting, like all immediate satisfactions of the flesh, is subject to a moral law of diminishing returns. It is a principle of biology and psychology that with a repetition the effect of a stimulus tends to decrease. In order then to produce the same effect as at first, the stimulus must be increased. Satisfaction will not long remain at one plateau. With petting, in order that the individual may continue to derive a given degree of satisfaction, the amount and intensity must be increased. However, there are serious limitations upon this process. Petting cannot be increased in intensity indefinitely; it cannot even be increased very much without the danger of getting beyond the control of the will.

At first, the more one gets the more one wants. Then after a point, the more one gets, the less the satisfaction. There comes a place where the satisfaction is not worth the effort and cost. It then takes on the aspect of something that is crude and disgusting, a shopworn thing. One will turn away from it as quickly as he first turned to it. The short-lived pleasure is too costly. The blessing is seen to be a burden. One may even become aware that such a process of satiety and revulsion is going on inside the other person. There is a sense that both of them are losing far more than they are gaining. If their relationship is one they both want to continue, they may ask themselves not "What are we getting out of this now?" but rather, "What are we getting out of this both for now and for our future lives?"

Revulsion is a powerful deterrent. It makes the spirit sadly conscious of its bondage to the flesh. No value remains from the petting since the only value sought was physical, while the sense of spiritual dignity and self-respect has declined with the realization of what was exploited to the neglect of all the superior values. Each partner in this petting affair will come to resent this turn of events. As John Macmurray sums it up: "The integrity of persons is inviolable. You shall not use a person for your own ends, or indeed for any ends, individual or social. To use another person is to violate his personality by making an object of him; and in violating the integrity of another you violate your own." Furthermore, as A. D. Lindsay says, "If we let outselves use other people or things as means only, we soon become grossly insensitive as to their quality."

This is something of the price of petting that every Christian young person must face in his or her own soul, and for the sake of his or her own future. A girl may still say, "What have I to lose?" The answer is: "A lot! The edge of your charm for one thing, and for another the joy of having saved something very precious for its proper time and place. You will have cheapened something of great worth by readily giving it to another without preserving its quality in a responsible commitment of love and marriage."

Sex always lies close to the surface of all male-female relationships. It can always be called forth to intensify a relationship between the sexes. The more it is given expression within an exclusive relationship between two persons, the more that relationship tends to fixate on a sexual level. The accent is on the wrong place! The relationship of growing love must place its chief emphasis upon the social not the sexual if it is to develop properly and fully.

More than once a fellow has seriously related himself to a girl, leading her to believe he desired to marry her. In the course of their relationship he was insistent upon their petting. The girl who had strong convictions against petting gave herself to his wishes on the premise that this was going to eventuate in their marriage anyway so it was not too bad. Soon she became habituated to petting, knowing now what it was to be aroused. Then without warning the fellow suddenly drops her and seeks to win a girl who will have nothing to do with petting. The fellow says to his male friends: "This is the kind of girl I have always dreamed I would marry." The non-petter? Yes. But he was the one who insisted on the petting before, drawing the first girl into it. Right! But his ideal and his compulsive behavior were in conflict.

The first girl compromised her ideal for his sake, only to lose him.

Petting often gets started in a very innocent way. A date is unplanned, and the two find themselves with time on their hands and nothing to do. They are alone and they are bored. With no common interests to provide at least a stimulating discussion, and no planned activity, it is an invitation to petting. At least this is one pleasurable thing they can do together to relieve the boredom. It requires no intelligence and is no challenge to personality. Like a game, it just starts when there is nothing better in view. But how soon the innocent game becomes a compulsive thing when passions have been aroused!

A fellow may easily rationalize his petting on the premise that there is nothing better to do, when in fact he deliberately did nothing to think through and plan a date around some worthwhile activity. He wanted only to pet, and so justified it.

A girl who has fallen victim to one unplanned date may well afford to inquire the next time what the fellow's plans are when he invites her out. And a thoughtful fellow will not only plan the date, but will invite the girl by asking if she is free to do this or that, specifying what his plans are. He certainly will not simply ask; "What are you doing tonight?" She may well reply: "That all depends; what do you have in mind?"

There are obviously situations where one would feel most uncomfortable not to indulge in some love-making. The simple solution, more workable than supposed, is just not to get into such situations.

An earnest young couple should plan to avoid the situations of solitude in a parked car on a lover's lane, idleness, or close proximity in some pre-selected dark and isolated spot. They should also watch for that moodiness in themselves that readily yields to lower ideals than are usually held.

Persons with specific skills are the most likely to have successful dates. It is the part of wisdom for an individual to develop skills in a variety of activities and pursuits. Quite generally this goes hand in hand with a variety of personal contacts rather than with limited associations. If one only can think of what he is missing by refraining from petting, and dwells upon his impulses to pet, the problem will be magnified for him over what it would be if he used his mind to think of the wide number of interests that would challenge his thought and skill. The best thing is always the displacement of habitual sex-thinking by other strong interests. A good question for young people, who have become involved with each other, is to ask: "Do other activities beside petting tend to make our relationship boring and frustrating, or rich and meaningful?" Also, "Do we have anything truly worthwhile and meaningful in our relationship beside the pleasure of petting?"

Two different reactions illustrate the complications of petting. A fellow declares: "I got so intoxicated with the thrill of petting, and so in love with the feeling of being loved, that I didn't really know what love was. So I never met the girl of my ideals; I was too occupied chasing the good petters." Like so many others, this young fellow discovered that he had an attachment based on compulsive sex interest, and this was sufficient to obscure for him the fact that they had few other interests in common.

Or take the case of the girl who inquires: "I can't understand it. After being out with my boy friend, for some reason I begin to cry. Sometimes I sob and sob for no reason at all and just can't quiet down. I'm not unhappy about him, so why should I cry?" Her crying was a method of releasing tension created by too much petting. Emotionally fatigued and sexually unsatisfied, this inwardly frustrated girl compulsively cried to relieve the emotional tension.

Petting that stops short of a climax will face the participants, especially the fellows, with the necessity of relieving that tension in some way. The common way is masturbation, another sexual act accomplished in secrecy, a furtive thing fraught with guilt feelings. This is the way of distressing injury to self-esteem and self-control. Just thinking about all of this sex activity will become all-absorbing. Struggling against thought-stimulation rendered vivid by habitual petting will draw off energies needed for concentration on other more worthwhile pursuits, such as study or creative work.

Most dates are relatively brief in time, so necessitate centering attention upon relatively few activities. If attention is focused upon petting, a false center is created which excludes the other possible experiences open to those who are seeking to know each other better. It excludes activities which afford greater rewards and satisfactions over a longer period of time. So petting tends to put the whole relationship on a restricted basis. It may exploit the one fact they are already agreed upon and nothing more.

Jesus said: " . . . whosoever looketh on a woman to lust after her hath committed adultery with her already in his heart" (Matthew 5:28). Lusting begins with looking. Or one might say that lusting can begin with imagining, for one can look through the eyes of imagination. It is this feature of moral evil that is not fully recognized by those who pet to a climax and then suggest that the moral quality of that act is not as bad an intercourse because it leaves the woman still a virgin! In such a case a man is actually "looking" through his hands and imagination, in fantasy violating the body of another person in a more thoroughgoing way than the man whom Jesus condemned as committing adultery in his heart because he merely looked on a woman to lust.

When two persons have progressed in their petting to the point of stimulating the sexual organs themselves, they must intuitively feel that the last barrier of sacred withholding has been passed. Even a meeting of the sexual organs would add little to the moral quality of their practice. There may be little conscious guilt when that barrier is passed, but guilt feelings will subconsciously be present. There is a moral monitor within, even though we may not consciously feel guilt. We do know when selfhood has been exploited and personal integrity has been violated. When the erogenous zones of the body have been manipulated by another, the same self-respect that would restrain one from publicly showing those parts of the body has now suffered a violation just as real, even though there is no public shame. Sensing that one's integrity has been violated comes soonest in superior persons, and certainly should come quickly in a sensitive Christian for whom this is a hallowed matter, for whom there is a true sense of the sanctity of sex.

Persons can touch in many ways; they touch with hands, arms, lips. They can touch by kissing, hugging, caressing. They can also touch with thoughts and imaginations, with letters or photographs. We say commonly "Let's keep in touch."

Now any act is what it is because of its meaning to the persons involved. Thus two persons engaged in petting can hardly say with honesty that there is less meaning than in actual intercourse, for mentally they have touched with the most intimate meaning. By touch and imagination they have invaded the inmost precincts of each other's personal and sexual being. The bodily secret of both has been revealed. Actual intercourse would add little beside the possibility of pregnancy. So one must conclude that the Christian view of petting is to put it on the same moral level as intercourse itself.

There is a vastly different quality to the light touch of sitting close, holding hands, or fingering something like one's watch or necklace. To walk with arms entwined, to give a light kiss—these are soon over, leaving a pleasant and exhilarating memory of affection expressed, yet with neither person aroused to a strong sexual demand. Nothing sacred about one's body has been violated. These expressions seldom lead to a sense of shame or to loss of self-respect.

In contradistinction, those acts of petting which progress in the direction of awakening erotic impulses and arousing sexual demands are in another category altogether. How much better to preserve love's full force intact until the time when it can be a unique self-giving to the object of one's devotion in the permanent relation of marriage. Then when problems and crises come in later life, and the two face them together with courage, faith, and mutual trust, it will be found easier, inasmuch as they discovered the fullness of love together in that marriage, and they know what it is to have sacrificed immediate possibilities of pleasure for the greater benefits of finding their joys in the marriage commitment.

Petting makes common and vulgar what God intends to be noble and pure. The greatest value of kisses and caresses is that they are unique and precious gifts reserved for the beloved alone. They are given when they can lead fully to satisfaction and well-being. So really petting is playing at love in such a way as tends to make the more genuine expressions of love seem dull, stereotyped, and unsatisfying. The finer sensitivities of true love are dulled. Many a young woman has failed to recognize true love in a properly restrained lover because her experience of intense petting prompted the false expectation that a true lover would always be sexually aggressive and free to initiate familiarities.

Dr. Henry Bowman aptly illustrates petting with the analogy of the squirrel in a cage. The squirrel runs long and fast, only to stop exhausted, yet in the same place where it started, no further. Petting becomes cumulative, gathering emotional momentum as it goes on, but for all of its intensity it gets nowhere. In fact the squirrel is better off than the couple who tread the squirrel cage of petting, for the squirrel cannot experience the emotional exhaustion, the regret and disappointment, or the resentfulness that the couple may.

The two who have become highly keyed up under the emotional strain of petting are conscious of the fact, sensing that they are nervous, irritable, and tend to quarrel over inconsequentials. Their feeling is one of frustration, self-disgust, and may result in one deciding not to have anything further to do with the other.

Actually, what one dislikes is his frustration and emotional conflict, but he tends to identify this conflict with dislike for the other person. Resentfulness easily focuses upon the other person as though he or she were the cause of the disappointment. No wonder petting is a cause for the break-up of many a romantic relationship.

Dr. Peter Bertocci tells of a typical situation. The young couple have become habituated in their petting, only to realize at long last their predicament, and now no longer relish dates that they might have anticipated with enjoyment. They are now aware that all through the early hours of the evening each will be preoccupied with thoughts of what will happen when they finally get off alone. Only their petting seems important. Whatever the activities of the evening, they are bored in view of this prospect. Almost as soon as the date begins, the battle for composure and concentration on other things ensues. What was supposed to have been an evening of fun and getting to know each other in a social situation turns out to be an evening of tension and inner conflict. One's preoccupation even shows itself in one's inability to participate as keenly as he might in the group. He often betrays his remoteness to the social situation. Sex life has become a problem, and occasions for normal friendship with members of the opposite sex become psychological and moral battlegrounds. The young person feels that he is a problem not only to himself but to others. He loses self-assurance, and his guilt feelings incline him to feel that perhaps he is unacceptable to others as well. The very relation has come to depend for its success upon the petting that is now a compulsive demand. The whole tone of the relationship deteriorates because two people are enjoying only their least common denominator, their bodies. A date is only an occasion for the old routine, not for coming to know and share activities and interests. Ultimately the cost of such a relationship in terms of personal and social frustration will bring a crisis.

One of the greatest self-deceits is to think one is strong enough to be careless and not be harmed. But beyond self-consideration, the one who indulges in petting must answer not only for the stimulation of lust in one's own life, but for the unknown degree of lust, self-contempt, and spiritual defeat brought about in the partner.

For every Christian young person this is a decision in the realm of self-discipline with the help of the Holy Spirit. The Scriptures say: " . . . know ye not that your body is the temple of the Holy Ghost which is in you, which ye have of God, and ye are not your own? For ye are bought with a price: therefore glorify God in your body . . . " (I Corinthians 6:19, 20).

Whatever the standard of the non-Christian, the standard for the Christian is clear. His body is a sacred trust from God, its functions meant to be restricted to and preserved for the ends designed by God. Since petting is an unnatural function which substitutes for intercourse when intercourse is not appropriate, it is certainly not within God's will for a child of His.

This is not moralizing, but rather bringing the facts to bear in the interests of the happiness and well-being of those who are not yet in the position to evaluate the end results of petting for themselves.

Petting outside of marriage is sexual immorality, and Paul said distinctly: ". . . The body is not meant for immorality, but for the Lord . . . " (I Corinthians 6:13, RSV). Again, he said that a Christian must ". . . possess himself of his own vessel in sanctification and honor, not in the passion of lust . . . " (I Thessalonians 4:4, 5, ASV). To this is added the word of Peter: ". . . abstain from fleshly lusts, which war against the soul" (I Peter 2:11). And again, Paul's word to Timothy was: "Flee . . . youthful lusts . . . " (II Timothy 2:22). So the issues are clear and the decision is plain enough for those who are honest with themselves and with God.

It is the girl who must set the standard and apply the brakes. This is not always the easiest thing to do. For the girl whose problem is in knowing just how to say "no," perhaps a word will be of some help. Saying "no" is indeed a delicate matter, for a girl who is sensitive could never wish to embarrass her friend. So she will not act shocked or hurt, nor will she withdraw from him in a touch-me-not attitude. She will instead include herself with him in a positive approach, not making too much over it. She might well say, for example: "I'm fond of you Bill; let's just keep it like this shall we?" And this would not be a poor time to squeeze his hand in reassurance.

If Bill is approaching her in love and thoughtfulness, he will appreciate her expression and restriction. The way it was said and the squeeze of his hand will mean worlds more to him in that moment than the rejection of his petting impulse. They have met as true persons and established a point of relationship between them.

If Bill is only interested in petting, her word will not have been misplaced at all, nor will her reassuring squeeze of his hand. If petting was what Bill wanted most, her problem will not remain for long, for Bill will probably not give her a second opportunity to turn him down.

Norval Geldenhuys has stated it well: "Sexual experiences penetrate to the very depths of man's being. That is why sexual desire can lead to such sublime heights of joy, happiness and fullness when used correctly; yet when used incorrectly it can drag a man down to unfathomable depths of sin, impurity and misery. When put to any other use than that for which it was created, sexual desires have a diabolical power to ruin and pollute lives. The abuse of sexual desire causes Nature to take revenge by sowing destruction and havoc in the moral psychological and physiological life of the abuser. What the author of Proverbs 6:32 wrote concerning adultery is equally true of all other sexual abuses: 'He that committeth adultery . . . is void of understanding: He doeth it who would destroy his own soul.' "

Another warning from Scripture comes from the story of Tamar and Prince Amnon in the Old Testament. The prince in the court of David seduced a young girl and thought he had gotten away with it. But the Bible says bluntly: " . . . the hatred with which he hated her was greater than the love with which he had loved her . . ." (II Samuel 13:15, RSV). This is the bitter fruit that so frequently follows.

Now for a practical word or two before closing this chapter. The man and woman who are engaged and close to their wedding day will find caresses proper to a limited extent, but even then will recognize that though they are pledged to each other they should be careful not to frustrate their highest hopes and expectations by a short-circuited experience calculated to give them only frustration and disappointment. All sanctions and restrictions should be prayerfully agreed upon in the light of their future together, and as subject to the Lord in all things. They who preserve love's strength intact will know in God's time a love that will be beautiful, well-adjusted, full and free. They will experience a depth of satisfaction beyond their highest dreams. This is God's sure reward for the self-disciplined Christian!

The one who makes sex an end in itself, who determines to get all he can out of sex as sex, is driven into an endless pursuit. He seeks new experience, real or imagined, having tired of the latest exploitation. He is trying to find in sex what sex cannot give him. He only finds to his sorrow that in promiscuous petting it is true that familiarity breeds contempt.

Jeremy Taylor prayed: "Let my body be servant of my spirit, and both body and spirit servants of Jesus." Let every Christian young person take to himself this prayer!

We have said some things very plainly in this chapter because they are desperately needed by thousands of Christian young people today. Yet plain speech must be reverent, for this is a hallowed subject that must not be made common in any way. An assessment of what has been said shall not be the last word for any earnest young Christian. In the last analysis young Christians, like their seniors, must find their crystal clear guidance within the Lordship of Christ. Chapter ten will be concerned with the crucial matter of the Christian's personal liberty, and the Lordship of Christ that properly limits and directs that liberty.

9. MISCHIEVOUS BOREDOM

PERHAPS it seems out of place in a book on Christian concepts of love, sex, and marriage to have a chapter on boredom. Yet this enters in as a part of the practical aim of the book. It is the purpose of these pages to investigate problem areas in the dating structure as well as in marriage itself. We are seeking causes, and have already noted that infatuation is not infrequently the result of an attempt to break away from a drab and boring life-situation. Infatuation is sometimes motivated by the compulsive desire for excitement, for a new and novel experience, for something that will temporarily at least lift one out of oneself and one's colorless surroundings. Beside that, we have noted that petting often develops because young people have nothing better to do with themselves. Idleness and the challenge of leisure hours, lack of adequate lifegoals, and boredom all enter into needs that young people have today.

Erich Fromm commented that man is the only animal that can be bored. Surely it is doubtful that animals or idiots are ever bored! It seems equally certain from all reports that Christian young people generally are just about as often the victims of boredom as their non-Christian friends, perhaps more so in some instances than others who have found ways to utilize everything at hand for a full life.

Boredom has to do with the full occupation of one's faculties. Contrast the gangster who is not bored as he flees from the police, with the Duke of Devonshire who yawned during his maiden speech in the House of Lords! It is not so much what we are doing as what effect what we are doing has upon us. Does it not suggest that Christian young people can live full lives for Christ, and so occupy their faculties for Him and for His service as not to suffer from compulsions arising from boredom? Of course, they can choose to follow the Lord at a spiritual distance and live far from their ideal because of the reactions created by boredom or the fear of it.

The opposite of boredom is a life lived to the brim, not just in activity as such, but in creative activity. Productive lives are not bored lives. Again, this is to suggest that Christians have an infallible formula for counteracting boredom, and are of all bored people the least excusable. The full life in Christ is the solution to boredom.

Rollo May, the New York psychiatrist, said that boredom is the occupational hazard of being human. This is echoed by the Johns Hopkins Medical School professor who said that boredom is a far greater killer than heart disease or cancer. Dr. Abraham Myerson of the Department of Psychiatry at Harvard Medical School further adds: "The four horsemen of the weary spirit are: sorrow, fatigue, fear, and boredom." As we shall see, boredom is that weariness of spirit that results when man seeks incessantly to relate himself to transient, earthly satisfactions. Boredom is the emptiness that remains when the transient earthly pleasures are seen for what they really are.

Boredom is closely associated with imagination and memory. This brings to mind Thackeray's description of one who "having a lively imagination, mistook himself for a person of importance very easily." Imagination has the ability of contrasting present circumstances with supposedly more pleasant or excitable circumstances. By means of imagination a person can live in two worlds at once, the real and the make-believe. The make-believe world may be more vivid than the real for those whose imaginations are highly developed. And memory can feed imagination with materials from the past, so one can be bored simply by imagining oneself in more exciting situations and continuously contrasting them with his real life. Imagination, kindled by the memories of more exhilarating times past, if undisciplined can lead one into boredom. Imagination must be regulated by our life in Christ.

Boredom is also closely associated with frustration. How easily man is blocked and frustrated! He comes to fear the routines and limitations which threaten him with boredom. He resists by blasting away one entrenchment after another, his pent-up powers of freedom and progress ever seeking new avenues for self-expression. Yet, no combination of pleasures can ever exhaust the powers of his freedom or his creativeness. Momentary pleasures are limited and frustrating, whether they be forms of sex, gambling, acclaim, or whatever. Frustrated lives tend to deteriorate into boredom, indifference, and carelessness. It isn't the frustration that is so damaging as it is the boredom that one allows to take over the spirit as a result of frustration. Boredom is a thing of the spirit.

Boredom is closely associated with temptation, for it is out of inactivity and idleness that young people drift into things they know to be contrary to the will of God. Often the promptings of lower ideals which arise from boredom are stronger than the promptings which arise from knowledge of God's will. Boredom is surely fertile soil for temptation!

A rather different reaction, not less important, comes strangely from one's reaction to having chosen God's best. When a young person obeys the dictates of God and conscience, but finds no substitute for what has been relinquished, there may be resentfulness that such enticements are taboo. The vacuum may cause boredom as well as resentfulness. It is just as important to discern God's will in the matter of what should occupy us, as in the matter of what should not occupy us!

Boredom is closely associated with excitement. It is its opposite. The desire for excitement is deep-seated in us all, especially in men. It is one of the chief gratifications of the self-life; it feeds the emotional side of man. Because our day is so largely absorbed in exciting entertainment and activity, we have become the land of the great Ho-Hum. Strange that we could live in a land that produces so many things for the purpose of alleviating boredom, and yet be probably the most bored people on earth!

We are perhaps less bored than our ancestors were, or at least have less reason to be bored than they, but surely we are a generation more afraid of boredom. Our periods of boredom at least seem more intense and more damaging, perhaps in part because we have come to believe that boredom is to be avoided like the plague.

Bertrand Russell has written: "Boredom is therefore a vital problem . . . since at least half the sins of mankind are caused by the fear of it." So many of our daily pursuits are unconsciously motivated by the fear of boredom.

Man is fickle and moves impatiently from one momentary satisfaction to another. One pleasure collapses only to be supplanted by another. Each satisfaction will be pursued for a time and then a reaction sets in. Saturation or satiety, the law of diminishing returns, or exhausted emotions will drain away interest and pleasure. When hopes have been placed in temporary and immediate pleasures and are found false, a person may give up hope for the time, and in doing so become bored, indifferent, and careless. He can regain his hope and conquer boredom when he locates those abiding satisfactions for which his free and creative spirit can live and die without regret. Is it not easy to see how this relates to finding and marrying the right person? Is it not easy to see the peril of relating oneself to a person whose attractiveness may be just an exciting personality or body?

Among Christians, as with others, the higher the income bracket the greater the tendency to pursue excitement and pleasure. The things that money can buy are largely devoted to creating pleasure, excitement and diversion. Persons with higher incomes have greater opportunities and usually more leisure time to fill the life either with creative activity and interest, or with boredom.

The ideal of the man of the world includes freedom from boredom. It is the ideal which says that if one can only keep everlastingly busy and "on the go," one will evade boredom successfully. It is a false ideal, but many young Christians assimilate it to themselves from the advertising and entertainment media of the day. It still goes, however, that the morning after will probably be as boring as the evening before was exciting.

In dating, young people often find that highly exciting activities end in a highly boring aftermath. Excitement can never be the basis for successful dating. In this same connection it could be shown that exciting Saturday evenings are poor preparation for the less exciting though more real pleasures of the Lord's day. A wonderful opportunity is afforded by the Lord's day for physical rest, mental repose, and spiritual enrichment. The day might be well employed in turning away from the insistence of the world that everyone should join in the excitements and entertainments which end only in boredom and the sense of time and energy squandered.

Into the middle class population especially has come the effect of a new form of pleasure and excitement, television. Within a few years it has entrenched itself so as to seem to most persons a necessary part of existence. Television in every living room now simulates the realities which only the better-heeled once enjoyed in person.

One can flip on the TV and immediately be transported to a night club, identify oneself with all that is going on, and thus enjoy vicariously what one might never think of participating in personally.

If one gets bored with the night club, its drinking and dancing and sophisticated personalities, it doesn't involve even so much as leaving the place and driving elsewhere; one merely turns the dial again and presto! one is at the ringside for the main event. One may then wind up tighter than a corkscrew in identification with a favored fighter. And if the fight turns out to be dull, simply flip the dial again; there is always a red-hot thriller on the late show. If one has had a boring day, this will help one forget, and will provide the emotional exhilaration absent in one's routine day. When the evening is over, weariness will cause worry to evaporate and sleep will come to erase another day.

In an average home in an average evening, without ever budging from one's chair, one may run the gamut from a side-splitting comedy to a violent murder to a chokingly sentimental love play, ending up with an hour at the Stork Club and ten rounds of fights. All in one evening! And this in perfect privacy, away from the demands of people and the challenging pursuits of a creative nature. Then one takes it all to bed to be the most vivid part of one's mental activity during the night hours when the body rests—or tosses.

Television comedy, violence, or even games may provide a temporary escape hatch from pressing boredom at the moment. But in the end of all such activities we must come back to ourselves, our own lives and world. Often the only value remaining is the sense of time wasted and ourselves less prepared for the challenge of tomorrow.

No wonder young people, weaned on such excitement, expect their love affairs to be of the celluloid type, exciting adventures filled with intense pleasures at little or no cost! How are they to understand that marriage is to be creative, that creativeness costs, when they see nothing else in life that depends upon creativity? Creativeness no longer seems to them to have anything to do with pleasure, so why should it in dating or in marriage?

It is all part of the great American game, this flight from the land of Ho-Hum. Even the salaries of entertainers run into the millions if they can help us accomplish the flight from boredom.

The unconscious flight from boredom which affects us all to some extent is illustrated humorously by the bus driver in Brooklyn some time back who drove away in his empty bus and was picked up in Florida. He had a long, excellent record with the company. When he returned there was a crowd to cheer him; he was a hero in Brooklyn! Why? Because others saw themselves identified in spirit with him.

It is the flight from boredom that makes the never-never land so appealing. And it is this flight that is compatible with infatuation and the unrealities of romantic marriages which are the outcome of infatuation. Wherever there is evidence of a strong tendency toward boredom and the attempted flight from it, a person in love may well take caution. All the more should that one base the selection of a mate upon mutually creative interests, the most solid guarantee of lasting happiness.

In happy contrast to boredom in human experience,

we read of our Lord Jesus Christ. With every shade of human experience touching His life, there is never a hint that He was ever bored. But then how could He be? For the business of Christ is life, real life, full life! Life is the very opposite of boredom; it is only simulated life, unreal life, that corrodes one's experience and produces boredom. Jesus said: " . . . I am come that they might have life, and that they might have it more abundantly" (John 10:10). The abundant life has no relevancy to the bored life! To concern ourselves with His program for our lives will be to break through the causes for boredom and lead on to the abundant life which He alone can give.

Boredom is thus seen to be related to sophistication and superficiality. In many ways this is the product of our culture. For one thing, the exaggerated importance we attach to time-savers is to be compared with the little importance we attach to what we may do creatively with the time we save. Time-savers are only useful as they free individuals for creative enterprise. They only contribute to boredom where there is no accompanying vision of creative opportunity. And Christian people are those who have been called to live realistically and creatively and sacrificially to serve the ends of the gospel in a desperately needy world. No Christian should earn the epitaph: "Died of old age at 21."

Most excitement comes to us today as passive individuals. We do not actively participate in activities as once was the case. Our only activity, as someone has suggested, seems to be the frantic movement of trying to get away from it all! We have become a nation of spectators. The enormous sports program of America depends upon a few participants and millions of spectators. It is the same in the realm of entertainment. With millions working as cogs in the machinery of huge, sprawling industries, there are few who are creative in their economic lives.

But the true value of life must be worked for, and they demand personal creativity. Likewise, marriage must be a creative function; it cannot be merely something enjoyed passively as though the two partners were spectators of themselves. Marriage failure is frequently the result of expecting something for nothing. Not a few unhappy couples have discovered in marriage that with all of their spectator interests they were not proficient in creating real-life values.

One phase worthy of notice is that excitement is the generation of emotional energy. Emotional energy is released when excitement affects our metabolism, and the glands overact to meet emergency needs. But if there is no emergency and no need to act in an extraordinary way the energy is not put to work; it accumulates, and brings on nervous tension and often irritability. The energy is dammed up within. To be continually excited and to produce energy that is not expended will bring about a state of emotional exhaustion. Much of the fatigue that disturbed individuals complain about is simply emotional exhaustion.

How much better is a quiet walk, a worthwhile discussion, a creative hobby, an exhilarating recreation! How superior for young people to spend time getting to know one another better in such activities, than to spend it always in exciting spectator pursuits! Some excitement is good, of course, but not nearly so much as countless young people think they require. This means that for Christians to date successfully there must be ingenuity in the planning of dates. It is challenging to seek Christian substitutes, activities where the three basic requirements for a full interpersonal experience are to be realized. These three are: fellowship, recreational participation, and service.

Our competitive society enhances the problem of boredom by a great deal. Our competition is in the facets of our economic struggle, but a man doesn't leave the competitive life at his office when the work hours are over. Our culture emphasizes social competition. To add insult to injury, often between the economic competition of the day and the social competition of the evening, there is the competitive driving required even to get home!

In the last analysis, quarreling with the neighbors, gambling at the track, drinking at the bar, persecuting the employees, driving recklessly through town, and even wars can be little more than a reaction against the threat of boredom. Crime, violence, and suicide sometimes have no obvious cause other than boredom, the symptom of deeper personality and life problems. For greater numbers of persons, fortunately, it is sufficient to daydream.

The real tragedies occur when we discover our pursuit of excitement and subsequent flight from boredom have caught us unprepared for the more important quests in life, such as selecting our life partner and forging a successful marriage.

An individual must ever be growing toward something important, or he will turn to morbidity and despair, and finally to destructive activities. Boredom is a warning signal that we do not have adequate goals before us.

The alternation between excitement and boredom is an avenue to bad health. Our physical and emotional health must be sound if we are to make life's highest choices aright. Our bodies and spirits belong to God and are temples of the Holy Spirit. Our bodies and spirits are trusts from God. So the kind and the amount of emotional excitement permitted in the Christian's life must be discovered through prayerfully seeking the will of God. Certainly it will not be enough merely to regulate the kind and amount of excitement by what one thinks is necessary to hold a date!

There are two ways to destroy God's gifts: use them too much, or use them not at all. There is a sane and spiritual balance between the two extremes. The solution to boredom is not in repression but in regulation, not in free expression but in purposeful expression.

The Christian of all persons ought to know that there are seasons of activity and excitement and pleasure, even as there are seasons of the soul. Great books do not sparkle from the first page to the last, nor do great men achieve except as they have periods of quiet and inactivity. The most profitable work is often quite monotonous.

The Christian should learn to use periods of inactivity, not for boredom, but for creative rest, for thought and prayer. Spiritual meditation is an avenue open to all Christians for genuine recreating of energy. Proper inactivity can refresh, whereas the inactivity of boredom only fatigues.

Christians who are always in either a state of excitement or boredom, either very high or very low in their moods, are like cut flowers in a vase. They ave no creative roots in life; they are swept along by the superficial things of life.

For the Christian there must be an alternation between the active and the passive phases of life, an adjusting to the divine rhythm of life. There will be times for service and times for quiet devotion, times for speaking to God and times for listening, times for the expenditure of energy and times for the recuperating of energy. To learn and accept and utilize God's way is to be fortified against boredom and the misbehavior that so frequently results from it. This is but an extension of the principle of Sabbath rest, of creatively resting in the

Lord without busyness, or deadlines, or compelling activities of any sort. How difficult this is in modern life, but how necessary! By contrast, boredom is restless and destructive inactivity.

Logan Pearsall Smith once said: "What a bore it is, waking up in the morning always the same person!" This is really at the heart of man's boredom: his self-absorption. Whenever he is thinking about himself, lost in himself, he is bored; whenever he is not thinking about himself, he is not bored. It is the self-centered life that is subject to boredom. This should not surprise us at all, for we have been finding right along that the core of every personality problem, whether individual or in marriage, is self-centeredness. The father of anxiety, frustration, discontent, or boredom is self-absorption.

Boredom requires self-absorption to live and thrive. Freud said that man wants most of all be be loved, Jung that he wants most of all to feel secure, and Adler that he wants most of all to feel significant. These are fine distinctions in the general condition which Karen Horney points out in showing that man wants to be God. Man wants to be the center and the sovereign of his world.

Of equal importance is man's suspicion that he isn't God after all. As Rollo May puts it: "The chief problem of people in the middle decade of the twentieth century is emptiness." This is precisely what the preacher in Ecclesiastes meant when he said that all was vanity. Man is all puffed up, but empty inside. He is made of straw. To realize this is often to retreat into a state of boredom. Boredom is man's disturbance with the emptiness of his real life and his failure to know what to do about it.

We have characterized man's self-centeredness in its destructive capacity by the word "selfishness" (a word Presbyterians coined, by the way, about 1640. At least we Presbyterians have created something significant!). This selfishness is vividly portrayed by Albert E. Day in the following description: "Edith was a little country bounded on the north, south, east and west by Edith." We might add that boredom results from living in such close confinement!

Bertrand Russell takes the same approach, saying that the thing that bores us is "the intolerable sameness of the object of our devotion!" Surely we are bored because we live for ourselves in a little world of self-devotion. Thus the selfishness that enters into mate selection, or into marriage itself, will have one fatal consequence: one gets what one wants only to discover that what he got will not support his ego or fortify his selfishness. Marriage based on selfishness will turn to boredom.

Boredom always betrays purposelessness in life. This is an incipient disease among college students who cannot concentrate on their studies. As President Robert Gordon Sproul of the University of California said in a commencement address some years ago: "The trouble with most young people today is that they aim at nothing—and hit it!"

When there is lack of an adequate goal, there can be no true and powerful incentive in life. And without incentive, boredom will invade the personality. Again, it is symptomatic of the emptiness of much of modern life, the emptiness of people who are strangely very busy. Even in the life of a Christian young person there may be spiritual emptiness and purposelessness, hence extreme self-centeredness and boredom. How many Christian young people haven't matured any farther than the girl who despairingly blurted out: "I'm just a collection of mirrors, reflecting what everyone else expects of me!"

It is easy in our day for an individual to have his life regulated by anonymous authorities instead of by chosen goals. When this is the case, marriage will reflect something that was thoughtlessly drifted into. Aimless leisure and a life with inadequate goals provide fertile soil for an aimless marriage.

In his idealism, every intelligent Christian young person will seek a task to dignify his days. Early we perceive that there is no worse self-condemnation than comes of doing nothing worthwhile. Michelangelo said: "It is only well with me when I have a chisel in my hand." Young people who have known the benefits of wealth, who have had things given to them freely, are poor marriage risks if they have not learned the cost of things worthwhile to themselves. One must learn the dignity and wholesomeness of toil, the necessity of investing oneself in worthy tasks.

An uninvested life becomes a pathetic thing. Observe the active people who retire only to wither away and die from their boredom. Or see mothers whose children have grown up and moved away, who have only a sense of uselessness at the heart of their boredom.

George MacDonald said: "Nothing makes me feel so strong as a call for help." And nothing takes away boredom like the giving of oneself to a worthy task. For those who are dating and serious about possible marriage ahead, it will be worthwhile to take an inventory as to the extent each may be bored with life generally, or especially bored with each other when engaged in something other than loving each other. They might well ask themselves: "Are there mutual goals and interests sufficient to challenge our best when we are together? Have we adopted mutual goals that concern our dedication to Christ and our service for Him?"

The principle has been stated that no man can be himself until he gets out of himself and into work with which he identifies himself. One must lose himself in music really to enjoy it; one must forget himself in a

game to love it; one must identify himself with his loved
one in marriage if he is to have the pleasure of its benefits. As Gordon Allport has put it: "Paradoxically, self-
expression requires capacity to lose oneself in the pursuit of objectives not primarily referred to the self."
Whether it be in individual life or in married life, one
must find himself in the objectives which are outside of
and larger than himself. We have stated it before, and
we state it again here: Each for the other, and both for
Christ!

Christianity is a secret companionship. The joy and
purpose that derives from one's personal fellowship
with and obedience to Christ is a far superior incentive
in life than all of the excitements and pleasures this
world can contrive. There is an exhilaration and genuine excitement just in walking through life's dull places
with Him, and that of a sort that has no diminishing returns, no end in despair and boredom. Christ makes us
feel tall in His presence. Devotion to Him and service
for Him is of eternal worth. Blessed are those who experience this together in the bonds of Christian marriage!

If boredom is a spur, used of the Lord for the purpose of revealing our false pursuits, it is a good thing.
The Lord can use boredom as a means of bringing us to
Himself and to those purposes which are abiding, hence
satisfying rather than boring. Those who walk in fellowship with Christ will find it difficult to settle for less than
the best!

10. LIBERTY OR LORDSHIP?

MILTON had acute insight when he wrote: "None can love freedom heartily but good men; the rest love not freedom but license." Paul wrote to the Romans: "There is none that doeth good." The Scripture teaches that all men have by nature a passion, not for true liberty, but for license! It is only the redeemed person who is set free to live in liberty. But the problems do not evaporate simply by virtue of the fact that one becomes a Christian. Our day discloses the sad fact that the subject of Christian liberty is seldom held in Scriptural balance. The bias of sinful nature within the redeemed person tends to one or the other of two extremes.

Those who make too much of Christian liberty carry it to the extreme of license. The result is a life subject to no proper boundaries, an unregulated life. The end is moral anarchy and spiritual chaos!

Those who make too little of Christian liberty carry it to the extreme of legalism. The result in this instance is personal bondage to an arbitrary system of "Do" and "Don't." The end is a life largely negative and known mostly by its restrictions.

Both legalism and license are dreadful impostors. The Christian life is neither that of unregulated liberty, nor that of arbitrary rules. At the heart of the matter is a paradox: Liberty can only be defined in terms of its limits. Does this sound strange? Yet it is true. Liberty must be defined in terms of the purpose for which it exists or is desired. Freedom is never merely for freedom's sake alone. The essential condition of freedom is its end-purpose. This is to say that one is only free who consents to the proper limits of liberty. One is free insofar as one fulfills the purpose for which liberty is gained. This paradox is beautifully expressed by Felix Adler: "Binding ties are welcome insofar as they are necessary to unbind what is highest in us."

Man tenaciously clings to an illusion of personal freedom. He thinks he is running his life the way he wants to. He thinks he is free to do as he wants. Little does he perceive that this is the clue to his bondage. Here is suggested a workable definition of sin: "Sin is wilful independence from God."

Inherent in human sinfulness is the fact that proud ego has assumed the mastery. Does not every manner of sin come as the direct result of the presumption of a personal freedom from God? Is not every sin related to man's illusion that he is free to do what he pleases? Presumably free from all authorities, proud ego becomes its own authority. But such mastery is only bondage of a most sinister sort. The goal of man's salvation is to displace this sort of freedom with another, to exchange the liberty within the lordship of proud ego, for liberty within the Lordship of Christ.

From the nature of God and His unique place in the universe, He must be absolutely sovereign and absolutely free. God knows no limits to His liberty save His nature and truth. From the nature and place of man, he cannot be absolutely sovereign or absolutely free. Nothing is really free from Him who made it and set it within His purposes. Just ask yourself where such freedom is to be found outside of God.

The stars haven't got it. The stars are appointed to their orbits; perfect freedom for the stars would mean the destruction of the solar system. The ocean hasn't got it. The ocean is bound by shores and tides; perfect freedom for the ocean would upset the whole balance of life conditions on earth. And man hasn't got it. He is hemmed in by other men in his society. Man is one of the purposes of God, and can know liberty only within that purpose. He has liberty only within his relation to God above and man about him. He cannot drive his car any way he wants to, nor can he dispose of his garbage any way he wants to! His liberty is within certain prescribed limits. Liberty is always defined by its limits. The purpose of liberty is always the limit of liberty; this principle is basic to any understanding of the nature of liberty.

Every detail of man's life is conditioned by factors within and without him. Outwardly, his life is largely determined by what we call "circumstances." The word is a compound of "circum" which means around, as in circumference, etc., and "stance" which is what a baseball player assumes at the plate: he takes a stand. So the word means "things that stand around"! We are limited by the things that stand around, the circumstances of life.

Inwardly, a person's life is limited by attitudes, desires, etc. More than any one of us realizes, all persons are subject to inner compulsions that assert a mastery over the will as well as over the mind. Emotion often has a stronger power than reason.

So all men are under a master; either proud ego is lord, or Christ is Lord. As Paul puts it in Romans 6:16, "Know ye not, that to whom ye yield yourselves servants to obey, his servants ye are to whom ye obey?" All Christians are yielded Christians; they are yielded either to proud Self or to Christ.

Two illustrations, one from the Old Testament and one from the New will give real point to this truth. Israel had the illusion of freedom during the period of the Judges. It was a terrible time of anarchy and inconceivable bondage. It was described most aptly in these words: " . . . there was no king in Israel, but every man did that which was right in his own eyes" (Judges 17:6).

In the New Testament, recall the prodigal son who sought his freedom. The more he got what he wanted, the less he wanted what he got. His freedom led to famine and futility. Then an awesome moment arrived and he realized his liberty was an illusion! It was only a new form of the old bondage. His gains proved to be losses. He decided to turn his feet homeward, there to find true liberty in the father's house. This is well expressed in a French proverb: "He is not escaped who drags his chains."

Scripture declares both a glorious liberty for the one who is in Christ, and also the limits which give purpose and meaning to that liberty. Referring to the Law, Paul said, "Stand fast . . . in the liberty wherewith Christ hath made us free, and be not entangled again with the yoke of bondage" (Galatians 5:1). Now, free from the requirements of the Law for salvation, the one in Christ goes on to see how his liberty in living is limited. Three Scriptures will help us to see this truth:

(1) "If the Son . . . shall make you free, ye shall be free indeed" (John 8:36). Liberty is being in right relation to the Saviour. Liberty is within the Lordship of the One who bought us. It is liberty from the penalty and guilt of sin. It is also liberty from the necessity of a self- and sin-ruled life. Christian liberty is limited by the conditions of a vital union with Christ the Lord of all.

(2) " . . . where the Spirit of the Lord is, there is liberty" (II Corinthians 3:17). Every true believer is indwelt by the Holy Spirit; this is one of the chief provisions of God to ensure the quality and growth of the

believer's life. Liberty is experienced in the life that is limited to the leading of the Holy Spirit.

(3) " . . . the truth shall make you free" (John 8:32). Liberty is limited by truth, and truth accords with the nature and purposes of God. For God is true; the will of God and the truth of God are one and the same thing, but two sides of the same coin. Hence it follows that Christian liberty is within the limits of the character and purpose of God.

Liberty is never an end in itself, but a means to other ends. We are only free from something in order to be free for something. Liberty is not mere absence from restraint; it is the possibility of purpose! Liberty implies responsibility to some true purpose. So we must always ask two questions together: "What am I free from?" and "What am I free for?" Liberty is not the freedom to do what you want; it is the power to do what you ought!

This paradox is illustrated by Jesus' first sermon, when He said that He had come to set the captive free, and then immediately demanded: "Follow me." We sing it:

Make me a captive, Lord, and then I shall be free;
Force me to render up my sword, and I shall conqueror be.

God's Word safeguards liberty from abuse, and at the same time suggests the purposes regulating our liberty in Christ. I Peter 2:16 reads: "As free, and not using your liberty for a cloke of maliciousness, but as servants of God." Note the word "servants"; we are free in order to serve! Paul put this into practice, saying in I Corinthians 9:19: "For though I be free from all men, yet have I made myself servant unto all, that I might gain the more." Paul used his liberty to serve.

Service alone is not an adequate purpose. Galatians 5:13 reads: "For, brethren, ye have been called unto liberty; only use not liberty for an occasion to the flesh, but by love serve one another." Liberty is in order both to love and to serve! Or put in other words: liberty is limited by the demands of love and service. Anything that hinders our loving and serving destroys our true liberty.

What liberty the non-Christian has is really his willing bondage to sin, a bondage maintained by his love for self. By contrast, the liberty the Christian has is his willing bondage to righteousness, maintained by his love for Christ. Recall how Paul delighted to call himself "a bondslave of Jesus Christ," and Paul was of all men most gloriously at liberty. How this cuts away at the basic problem each one of us has, the attempt of proud ego to retain independence and its own lordship.

In making the application of Christian liberty and its limits to the specific matters of conduct which young people confront, a difficulty presents itself. Conduct is not a simple matter, but is as complex as life itself. Christian conduct involves right behavior in relationship to all things, not merely to a few obviously questionable things. Hence there can be no easy formulas, no pat answers, no ready-made solutions to fit all situations. The same decision will have different consequences under different circumstances. Let's briefly note the possibilities.

Some things are always right or wrong because of an inherent rightness or wrongness. Other things are either right or wrong according to their use, or according to the motive that lies behind their use. Some things are right up to a point, wrong beyond that point; this is the issue of moderation. Some things right in themselves are wrong by association. Some issues must be decided in terms of what is right or best for the individual making the choice, yet other issues must be decided in terms of what is right or best for the individual in this particular social matrix. All of this makes it quite evident that the Christian is governed not simply by a principle of liberty, but by liberty in relation to such other principles as moderation and discrimination.

Conscience is individual, and is subject to knowledge and growth through experience. The conscience of one Christian will never be precisely the conscience of another for the reason that conscience reflects the stage of maturity of an individual. It is for this reason that it is wholly improper for one Christian to impose the standard of his conscience upon another. A principle at the base of Presbyterian polity is an excellent commentary at this point: God alone is Lord of the conscience. Christian conscience must ever mature as it is corrected by the Word of God, cleansed through prayer, and controlled by the Holy Spirit.

Christian liberty is responsibility in action. The Apostle said: "But take heed lest by any means this liberty of yours become a stumblingblock to them that are weak" (I Corinthians 8:9). A young Christian may be expected to be enthralled with the new liberty that is his in Christ. It is also to be expected that with spiritual maturity there will come an ever-greater response to the limitations of that liberty. One of the loftiest expressions of the responsibility of liberty is that of Lowell:

> True freedom is to share
> All the chains our brothers wear.

Our paradox is given provocative expression by Augustine, who said: "Love God and do as you please." The implication is that if one loves God, one will please to do only those things which are motivated by that love. Translating this into our commitment to Christ, we might say: "Love the Lord Jesus Christ with all your heart, and do as you please." And so far as our relationship with others who are equally children of God and objects of Christ's redeeming death is concerned, we may add: "Love your neighbor as yourself and do as you please."

The Lord Jesus Christ was unquestionably the narrowest and broadest of all men. He was the freest yet the most responsible. He was the least arbitrary and legalistic, yet the most discriminating. He was as narrow as truth, as holiness, as the will of His Father. He was as broad as love, as compassion, and as the needs of Adam's fallen race. So must we be narrow yet broad, free yet bound!

The Corinthians had a serious problem of unregulated conduct. In writing to them, Paul three times repeated: "All things are lawful unto me." But this was no unlimited liberty he was teaching! Each time he followed the statement with "but . . . " and went on to limit the liberty. He agreed with them that they had liberty in Christ, but proceeded to correct their idea of liberty.

First, Paul set forth the principle of *personal progress*. "All things are lawful unto me, but not all things are profitable" (I Corinthians 6:12, lit.). A profitable life in Christ is built upon careful discrimination of what is profitable and what is not. Liberty will be limited by the choice of things profitable for personal progress for time and eternity.

Second, in the same verse, Paul set forth the principle of *practical authority*. " . . . all things are lawful for me, but I will not be brought under the power of any." Liberty is quickly destroyed whenever something freely indulged assumes the mastery. Habit-forming activities, those thing that lead to compulsive behavior, are wrong. Whatever asserts practical authority over the life of an individual is wrong. It may be the mastery of pleasure, acquisitiveness, security, prestige, recreation, etc.

Things good in themselves become wrong in one's life when they become controlling influences.

Thirdly, Paul set forth the test of *social responsibility.* " . . . All things are lawful for me, but all things edify not" (I Corinthians 10:23). To the Christians at Rome Paul said: "Let us . . . follow after the things . . . wherewith one may edify another" (Romans 14:19). It is not just a negative margin of safety that regulates liberty, but a positive purpose for good. Each Christian is made responsible not only for his own spiritual growth, but for that of others as well. For the sake of others whose weaker consciences might be offended by our actions, we refrain from some things and engage in others. True liberty in Christ is the very antithesis of selfishness. Even the things we might consider irrelevant or inconsequential are prayerfully discriminated as to whether they will or will not edify others whose lives we touch.

Granted, Christian liberty is limited by a supernatural standard of conduct. But thanks be to God, such Christian liberty may be fulfilled by a supernatural enabling! The Holy Spirit resides within the believer, and longs to preside over the liberty and purposes of his life.

James puts the paradox: "But he that looketh into the perfect law, the law of liberty, and so continueth, being not a hearer that forgetteth but a doer that worketh, this man shall be blessed in his doing" (James 1:25, ASV). True liberty in Christ will require as prime conditions a bent will, a broken ego, a disciplined walk, and a discriminating conduct! An earnest Christian young person will not take liberties with his liberty!

The issue before the Christian, then, is really not liberty but lordship! The only way to settle the issues of conduct in one's daily life is to enthrone the Lord Jesus Christ as absolute Lord of life.

We are Christians when by faith we take Christ as

our Saviour. But it is faith that takes Him for all that we know Him to be. The authentic confession of the early church is expressed by Paul in Romans 10:9 (ASV): ". . . if thou shalt confess with thy mouth Jesus as Lord, and shalt believe . . . that God hath raised him from the dead, thou shalt be saved." We cannot willingly take Christ as our Saviour and deny Him as our Lord at the same time. He is not received on the installment plan, as Saviour first and as Lord some time later. Nor is this some optional matter for just those Christians who choose to go on farther.

The great object of Christ's death and resurrection is not our salvation! The end-purpose is not our salvation; rather, our salvation is a means to the end that Christ might be enthroned as Lord over the individual's life! Romans 14:9 declares: "For to this end Christ both died, and rose, that he might be Lord . . . ." The intention of the Father is clear: the love that took Christ to Calvary intends nothing less than that He be Lord of all! Paul said to the same church at Corinth: "For we preach not ourselves, but Christ Jesus the Lord . . . ."

Christ as Saviour sets one free from the penalty and guilt of sin. Christ as Lord sets one free from the desires and dominion of sin. We are more than "believers" if we are to experience that liberty; we are "disciples." In every decision of daily conduct we need to hear His voice: "And why call ye me Lord, Lord, and do not the things which I say?" (Luke 6:46).

Can we afford to let Christ be Lord? Paradoxically, it is the limits that He sets upon our lives that make us free! And if He is Lord of all, He can make no mistakes!

What we have tried to say in this chapter is that Christian liberty is a precious benefit, but it is vital and meaningful only as it is limited. The principle of the New Testament might be put in this simple formula:

Liberty Limited by Lordship. The limits of liberty are purposeful, setting energy free and at the same time directing it to useful ends. The Christian young person who is seeking to know God's guidance in matters of dating conduct especially, may rest in the assurance that Christ is not taking away liberty or pleasure; He is regulating and directing one to the highest and most abiding pleasure and purpose.

> My heart is weak and poor
> Until it master find.
> It has no spring of action sure—
> It varies with the wind.
> It cannot freely move
> Till Thou hast wrought its chain;
> Enslave it with Thy matchless love,
> And deathless it shall reign.

11. COMMITTED!

FROM meeting to mating is a fascinating process! What's more exciting than a cloud built for two? It is a course of progressive commitment between two lovers. Courtship involves commitment of an intricate social physical, and psychological nature. From the start it is a commitment of time and interest. Engagement is not really the point of commitment; nowadays it is but the formal announcement of plans to marry.

One of the major problems brought to the counsellor today is that of broken engagement. In the majority of instances the serious factor is not the break itself, but the insufficient ground for having become engaged. Much that is usually relegated to the engagement period should properly be incorporated into courtship preceding engagement.

William James quoted the sage who remarked: "There is mighty little difference between one man and another, but what little difference there is, is mighty important!" We shall be concerned in this chapter to note some important differences bearing on marriage success, tracing the commitments of courtship through the engagement period. Special notice shall be given to the factors in broken engagement.

There comes that point in the courtship process when a couple becomes formally committed to marriage. This is announced at an appropriate celebration, a ring is customarily given, and the couple is "engaged." It's an age-old step in advance of marriage. But what does it really mean to be engaged? What valid purposes can be fulfilled by engagement? What aspects of the tradition are being modified in this mid-twentieth centry? Should engagements be broken ever? What is the desired length of engagement?

A troublesome factor is that engagement is an ill-defined affirmation of probable marriage only. It is socially vestigial, a much-modified survival of the old practice of marriage arrangement by the families of the betrothed. There is no true ritual save for the ring and the announcement party. There is uncertainty as to its duration, accomplishments, sanctions, even its fulfillment. Conception of its role in mate selection differs widely among the sociologists, and the Christian approach is still usually confined to the naïve idea: "Engagement is a pledge, and pledges must be kept." Such an extreme oversimplification is directly responsible for much distressing readjustment to broken engagement. Re-evaluation is overdue.

There are numerous types of engagements. Some are purely accidental; a young couple didn't really mean to commit themselves in a final way, but they were in each other's arms, the world looked beautiful and uncomplicated and all their own at the moment. Each was saying things in a crescendo of sentiment, and well—they heard themselves become engaged. And you just don't go back on pledges like that, you know!

Other engagements are habitual—the girl who doesn't feel right unless she's engaged, unless she belongs to some man and is deeply involved in "plans." Perhaps she feels the campus code considers her not yet mature if she hasn't been engaged at least once.

These are not valid engagements, but only the manipulations of opportunists and emotional dependents, for whom engagement is a dramatic incident adding zest to life-at-the-moment. Such persons are neither ready nor likely to marry. Some engagements do not even include plans to marry! They are merely prestige performances. Thrilling novelty and a mysterious new relationship is too much to turn down in the moonlight. There is no mutual decision to start solving problems together, but like a high school diploma it is an achievement, an end in itself. There is no commencement of preparation for greater responsibilities in family life, or full testing of personality for the adequacies requisite to working out a life together.

Still other engagements are entered into with the hope and confidence that a needed security will be added to the relationship. But engagement will never hold together what serious friendship cannot by itself hold together. Engagement is not intended to add security, but to express the security that already exists. Nor can engagement materially increase happiness, especially where two are looking to engagement to provide happiness they feel to be presently lacking. Security and happiness are both by-products of a right relationship.

Security actually is endangered somewhat by engagement because of the possibility then added for one to be jilted. Realistically, engagement is a gamble, one of life's calculated risks. It is a gamble that greater involvement will pay off in terms of actual marriage, and happy marriage at that. It also means a suspension of the selective search, and a commitment toward which family and friends may rightly be solicitous.

In the past, engagement afforded a period during which the couple thought only of getting ready for the wedding. The girl prepared her trousseau and planned the wedding, while the young man made necessary preparations for a home to which he might take his bride. It was assumed the wedding would certainly follow, for the man had made a solemn pledge. In fact, engagement was a promise to marry, constituted a legal contract in the eyes of the law. A broken engagement was as rare as a divorce, and if the engagement were broken by one against the will of the other, that one could be sued for "breach of promise."

Marriage was the chief career of women in generations prior to ours, and for a woman to be jilted was to jeopardize her career. Other men might consider her undesirable, the broken engagement being prima facie evidence that something was wrong with her. Society was set up to protect her against such an eventuality.

Formerly it was expected that the young man would make his intentions known to the father of the girl, and seek family approval in a formal way. Today it is quite otherwise. Parents, for all their concern, seldom feel they can so interfere as to ask a young man if he has "serious intentions." Nor do engaged couples feel they have made a legal contract when they agree to marry and become publicly engaged. Even the law recognizes more and more that engagement is a serious period of courtship with an advanced commitment rather than a legal contract or a binding pledge. Some states have outlawed breach of promise suits altogether.

If jilted, a young woman today has other resources so that she need not sit by the fireside nursing her broken heart and contemplating her ruined life. In the past quarter-century the meaning and function of engagement has undergone a radical change, so much so that many sociologists question its continuing function in the process of courtship. But despite shifting customs and conflicting conceptions, we believe there is a stable place for engagement, and a Christian use for such a relationship within the total courtship commitment.

Virtually everything assigned generally to the engagement period can with greater validity be assigned to serious courtship when two persons "have an understanding" they want to marry. But there is a psychological and a practical turn when a couple announce their intent and begin to make definite plans for the wedding day and the life together. So actually certain aspects ideally assigned to courtship, but usually lacking, are given a definite and more specific place in engagement.

Engagement is regarded today as the final factor in wise marriage choice. It is a period of courtship, the objective of which is settled and the consummation of which is now in view. It is a time during which the couple can make a careful check to see if they are well prepared to enter into the uncertainties of marriage with a well-based confidence and plan.

Engagement serves as an appropriate transition from the relative irresponsibility of single status to the responsible commitments of marriage. It is a time of specific planning and testing. Attention so largely focused previously on personality and background factors which have operated to draw the two together now focuses upon whether that relationship has adequate resources to weather the problems of marriage. Four principles gain major consideration: adaptability, communication, adjustment to reality, and the problem-solving and decision-making abilities.

Engagement thus brings a sobering realization of the closeness and seriousness of marriage and its impending responsibilities. The relationship becomes real to both the couple and their respective families as perhaps was not very real to them before. They can anticipate their new roles with more realism, experiencing the feeling of being almost married but not quite. As Burgess suggests, engagement is the psychological preparation for a radically different life. It prompts a rehearsal of many of the roles of marriage.

This familial review of the relationship during engagement is important. The families of the two have been largely spectators upon the developing association up to this point. Now they become active participants, seeking to know thoroughly (and sometimes to direct!) the pair. The two young people have terminated their seclusion in order to test their relation in broader ways, and a new dimension of problems is taken on. Family and friends shall watch closely now, forming and perhaps expressing judgments. The relationship is subject to influences and pressures as never before. But formal notice of intent has been given, family readjustment is granted time, full acceptance is sought.

A couple with a rather adequate courtship may nonetheless bring to engagement conflicting expectations of the roles they will play as husband and wife, as parents, and as members of the community. The extent to which these role expectations are merged will determine their chances for marriage happiness.

Adaptability depends upon communication, and communication involves the intimate sharing of common everyday experiences as fully as possible, evaluating skills necessary to married life, and fully discussing the range of matters before them. Perfecting their communication will enable the two to predict what the other will think and do in a variety of circumstances. Such predicting is a large part of adapting. The maturing relationship must show an ability to understand each other's needs and expectations. Individual goals must be merged, differences surfaced to see if they are basic and deep-rooted, and whether or not they are subject to adjustment. Engagement becomes the last chance to shed misgivings, and to test all the professions of affection which formerly put a halo over courtship.

Adjustment during engagement should be away from the overidealizations and toward realistic appraisal of the future mate. One's idealized view of himself must give way to a more mature and objective view of one's own marriageability. And perhaps the added commitment of engagement will encourage the girl to express more freely her aspirations in the marriage, the husband-to-be to express more freely his expectations of his wife as homemaker or career woman. He will determine more accurately the interest his bride will have in his vocation as economic considerations are taken into their plans. Views on family life, attitudes toward children, viewpoint on discipline, community aspirations, social and spiritual hopes—all will come into sharper focus.

Discussion of these many facets of married life tend to be somewhat subordinated during courtship; at least discussion then need not lead to decision. But during engagement, as Clifford Kirkpatrick points out, the relationship is psychologically stabilized by shifting from "if" to "when" in all their thinking. Now decisions are important. They involve the extent to which old friends will continue in the picture, the proximity of their new home to parental families, relatives that may prove difficult, probable earnings and how they will be managed, basic spiritual convictions, the adequacy of sex knowledge, and a thousand other items. This is the time to build a democratic approach to problem-solving functions, and especially to see whether one or the other attempts to dominate and reform his betrothed. Working together becomes the core of the relationship, seeing how the two work together as a team. Working and learning together take the place of the purely recreational pastimes. It is the time for solid projects and lasting hobbies and interests, time to associate more with people and to let other things come more and more into their life together.

Engagement is the best time to see how the relationship survives when temporary absences take place. Absences interspersed along the way are healthful experiences. Taking time away from each other for study or work is good in that it relieves the emotional intensity of being constantly together.

Today most engagements emerge gradually in the course of courtship, with few being able to say just when they became committed to marriage plans. Casual dating becomes serious dating and exclusive dating. This is followed by an informal understanding between the two based upon a mutual avowal of love. They understand that marriage at some time in the future is their settled hope. This is usually followed by a secret engagement shared with a few close friends and family members who are sworn to secrecy. Some time later a public engagement announcement is made, accompanied by notices and parties and the symbolic ring.

The ring as a symbol of a pledge comes from the ancient Egyptians, and has come down through the ages as the seal of marriage agreement. But changing attitudes have led to a new custom, that of exchanging fraternity pins or class rings. While this too is a form of commitment, it is usually considered representative of some sort of understanding between the two persons. It is generally regarded as not quite so binding as engagement, and hence may be dissolved much easier. And what is really suggested by this custom is that young people feel the need for some commitment of intent that is yet not so binding as engagement.

It seems generally that young people decide rather quickly that they are serious about turning a dating relationship into marriage. Usually this decision is made from within a few weeks to six months or so after they start seriously dating. Engagement is often the very next step after exclusive dating for several months, and one can only wonder how frequently it is a sincere desire to prove in some way that the intense affection shown has a responsible motive. It is a way of saying that this exclusive and intense relationship is not intended to be exploitative.

But this is overleaping an important intermediate step, that of "having an understanding." Such understandings are strong commitments which still leave open the possibility that, despite their sincere desire, the relationship may not wisely terminate in marriage.

Courtship should differ from dating in that the two are exclusively dedicated to this relation, and spend more time together in activities other than evening dates. They see each other in more varied real-life situations, learning what common interests exist, how their home backgrounds compare, and what elements of attraction are strongest.

How important it is during courtship that the two young people see each other in their respective homes if at all possible. If a young man sees his fiancée-to-be behave rudely or selfishly or irresponsibly around her own home, he may discover certain traits which would never make for happiness. The girl whose fiancé has always treated her as if she were a queen may be shocked to see how little thoughtfulness he has for his mother. Habitual behavior comes out most readily at home, especially if given a little time. True attitudes, likes and dislikes, and adjustment to family living are of crucial importance.

One danger of campus courtships is that they are contained within a narrow range. The college campus is far different from an average neighborhood. It is a far cry from home life. Campus popularity, academic activities, and family life irresponsibility easily make for an illusory idea of one's capacity for married life. On the campus of a Christian college one may act far differently than he would in a non-Christian environment. These are factors that must be duly considered.

Perhaps the single most important issue in selecting a

mate is personality need. This should be determined as accurately as possible before engagement. Studies disclose what seems reasonable to expect: namely, that a majority of personality needs, but not all, should be satisfied by the loved one. Since personality needs are complex, so the experiences of courtship should be broad enough to reveal these needs.

Before becoming engaged, as Evelyn Duvall puts it, "Make sure you are sure." This should be accomplished during the period when two persons "have an understanding." If the courtship is adequate, then the engagement period may be short. This will be discussed at greater length; suffice it merely to be mentioned at this point.

Two other matters which properly belong to the period of "having an understanding," but quite generally discussed as a part of the engagement, have to do with premarital counselling and physical examination. By what logic are these two phases delayed until the engagement has been announced? A serious young couple should take advantage of premarital counselling just prior to the intended announcement of engagement. If anything might be disclosed that would affect future planning adversely, it should be known during courtship. Out of the counselling session will come guiding lines for the all-important engagement period, and most importantly there may come advice against engagement.

The same logic dictates that premarital physical examinations be had just prior to the engagement announcement. At that time each one will be examined for inheritable disease, malformations, sterility, in fact for any physical cause that might disclose reasons for not marrying. This is doubly important when one realizes that there are those who entertain subconscious fears during engagement that something might be disclosed at the last moment that would disqualify them for marriage. Better to prevent such a possibility by planning an examination during courtship.

At some time in the love affair it seems appropriate to confess some elements of the past. It is natural for engaged couples, seeking true intimacy and oneness, to want to reveal everything to each other as a part of the communication required by love. The question of what to confess and when to confess it is highly charged and potentially disruptive. More than one engagement has been broken unexpectedly by a confession which brought a far greater reaction than could have been anticipated.

Burgess and Wallin found that former friends of the opposite sex was the topic that provoked the most "reticence, tension, or emotion" during engagement. Robert Blood wisely says: "With few exceptions the present engagement is best viewed as a new beginning which would only be handicapped by dragging in the details of previous relationships."

Landis suggests four questions one should ask before confessing something for which there is guilt feeling: (1) Why do I wish to tell? (2) Will our marriage be happier and more secure for the confessing? (3) Will my fiancée be happier? (4) If I must confess, is this the best person to confess to?

Taking these in order, it may be that one wishes to reveal the past simply to relieve a bad conscience. It may be a means of self-inflicted punishment to share it thus with a loved one. Or it may even be a compulsion to impress another, or to arouse attention of an anxious, pitying sort. Secondly, as to whether the marriage will be happier and more secure, this would suggest only confessing those things absolutely necessary to a true evaluation of marriage success and adjustment. That is, confess those things that would likely upset marriage adjustment if found out later. It is better to confess than to be caught, and thus expose oneself to undue suspicion regarding the whole relationship. It is doubtful that previous affairs should be brought up unless somewhere an extensive sexual experience was involved that had far more meaning than a chance experience. But here is a decision that must be made prayerfully before God.

A confession may wrongly arouse later suspicions, for it is of the order of things that become easily magnified in an individual's mind, lending exaggerated importance, and creating undue concern and unhappiness. Different people react differently to confessions, an insecure person being confronted with an adjustment that may possibly be too great to make.

This brings us to the fourth question: "If I confess, is the loved one the best one to confess to?" It is likely that more often than not the answer will be "No." Certainly, when in doubt, don't! Far better to go to a pastor or counsellor who can advise whether the confession ought to be made to the loved one.

Because of the emotional hypersensitivity during engagement, nothing should be confessed merely to obtain emotional release. Remember, the loved one will forever after carry the burden of that revelation.

Things which most surely should be revealed include any previous marriage, even if it was annulled. Hereditary defects, serious diseases or operations, and any defects that might make for not having children should be made known. Any history of venereal disease, heart trouble, tuberculosis, mental breakdown or psychiatric treatment should also be revealed. Any debts or similar obligations should be discussed.

It is the author's strong conviction that all such matters should be revealed and discussed just prior to engagement, not during engagement. We have traced the functional meaning of engagement as being a preparatory period just before marriage itself. This commitment of enagagement should not be made while there are evident areas of the relationship as yet unevaluated or unrevealed.

It is not wise to become formally engaged when the possible wedding date is so remote that the two cannot directly plan for it. Engagement should be a period of purposeful planning for the wedding and for married life just ahead. Decisions, saving and spending, interacting with each other's families, and carrying responsibilities should all directly relate to the married life before them.

When engagement must be prolonged and there is no greater objective than just to be engaged, the relationship is bound to create tensions. Engagement must be more than marking time with more love-making. Engagement is not a device to justify a more intense love-making, nor can the fact of engagement prevent a couple from simply losing interest. It should take place only when the two are ready for the definite stage of planning which immediately precedes marriage.

In our day, one problem of protracted engagement is being met by the fact that young women no longer demand a certain standard of living to be secured before they will marry. More and more there is willingness to help by working while the husband gets professional or other special training. It is true that middle-class parents are more inclined nowadays to continue their support of the married couple who face long educational careers. The prevailing idea is that of a partnership where the wife helps on the economic side, the husband on the domestic side. Increasingly college authorities are coming to regard this as a wholesome approach.

As to the length of engagement, there can be no specific formula. Much depends upon how long and how effective the courtship preceding engagement has been. These stages are not to be measured in terms of months or years but in terms of accomplished adjustments and depth of understanding. It is the length of the entire relationship and the extent to which it has provided a thorough acquaintance that is all-important. Obviously the time to get to know one another is before engagement. Then the engagement can move rapidly toward the marriage itself.

Some people can get well acquainted in a relatively short period of time, but it holds true that this is risky for the reason that it takes time for relationships, moods, skills, and stability to be measured. The danger is that young people will assume they know each other far better than they actually do. This is the price of immaturity and inexperience. On the other hand, there are those who are engaged for years who never settle major questions before them. Long engagement is no substitute for maturity.

In the past short engagements were considered desirable. Increasing freedom in expressing affection during engagement suggested the problem of premarital sexual intimacy, so the logical solution was to recommend short engagements in order that the couple might be ushered into marriage quickly and safely.

More recently, with the advent of sociological studies which make much of sampling, the trend became that of recommending long engagements. Investigators like Burgess and Wallin, or Terman of Stanford, showed the relationship of marital success with engagement of two years duration or more. It could be shown from their studies that high predictability of marriage correlated with engagement of five years duration! But two factors must be critically analyzed. First, many lengthy engagements are not intentional. Marriage is postponed because of such obstacles as military service or educational requirements. Secondly, the nature of engagement itself, when correctly evaluated, does not suggest that its function is of long duration. The same misunderstanding of the function of engagement accounts both for many long engagements and many broken engagements.

The hazard of the long engagement is the continued stimulation which affords no acceptable outlet. It is a mistake for couples to spend long hours together, night after night, with no interest other than themselves and their love-making. The hours, days, and months of engagement must have substance; just so much unadulterated love-making leads to boredom and to desperation. Protracted engagements can also atrophy. Lovers get on each other's nerves when there is exclusive preoccupation with themselves yet with no workable goals to demand their thought and ingenuity.

Engagement should be long enough to make sure you are sure, to plan the wedding and the necessary first phases of marriage such as where you will live, etc. It should be long enough to get family and friends used to your being one and to adjust to the fact. If the normal processes of courtship have not been adequate, then engagement should be lengthened correspondingly. If there has been an extended period of separation just prior to engagement, that engagemnt period should be lengthened to evaluate the effects of that separation. Emotional maturity is exceedingly important, but again let it be said that this should be evaluated before engagement, not afterwards.

The most practical advice seems to suggest approximately one year for engagement, with preferably two years or more of courtship preceding it. Today young people in an urban environment have more highly differentiated interests and objectives than were ever possible before. Longer and closer association is necessary because of this trend. Compatibility has many more faces today. It is probably true that a man who is willing to date a girl for a year or so and then be engaged for a year before marrying possesses other traits which indicate stability and a willingness to work through to the solutions of problems.

Let us consider some of the areas of conflict that may terminate an engagement. These are many and we shall deal with only some of the more common.

Conflict with each other's families may develop during engagement. Families can intrude by raising issues they think are important to the coming marriage, or by attempting to get the couple to prolong their engagement unduly. They may interfere in the actual planning of the wedding or the home, or they may offer to take part of the responsibility in a way not acceptable to one of the partners.

Long-standing friendships go through a change after engagement is announced. Engagement tends to weaken these friendships, inasmuch as time and opportunity for their cultivation is increasingly limited, and the focus of interest is elsewhere. These friendships may become sources of conflict if one should think his friend's engagement is to someone who fails to measure up to one's ideal set for that friend. The friends themselves may be guilty of jealousy, feeling they have a vested interest and going on to make an appraisal that may not be fair but subconsciously designed to break up the engagement in an effort to maintain the friendship.

Preceding attachments, especially if they involved engagement, sometimes carry over as emotional complications. One may not be thoroughly weaned away from the partner of a previous relationship, especially if the other was responsible for breaking it. Conflict may develop over comparisons made between the present partner and some choice of the past. Broken affairs in one's history frequently explain one's insecurity. They can account for one being sensitive to the point of exaggerating the possibility that the present love affair will also come to an end.

Differences in economic outlook may come to conflict when engagement brings the couple to the place of specific planning. This may involve widely discrepant ideas of spending, or the woman's questioning of the husband's ability to achieve an adequate economic status.

Heavy demands upon study or work, necessitated perhaps by the wedding plans or moving into the new home, may make it increasingly difficult for a couple to see each other as often as one or both may desire. This may precipitate a serious issue, and may reveal a flimsy base for engagement.

Sometimes the extent to which affection is to be displayed after engagement is a source of difference. And deeper is the problem of premarital intimacy and the sanctions that one may assume to be proper to engagement and to which the other disagrees. It is a common error to think that premarital intimacy will cement the relationship, when studies indicate that actually this is a reason sometimes reported for broken engagement. Because of the low quality of such experience, and the sense of guilt and frustration, disappointment may so cloud the whole relationship as to cause a broken engagement.

Quarrels are a common source of broken engagement. Now, a few quarrels may mean nothing except that the two are working through to solutions for sharply defined differences. On the other hand, frequent and intensive quarrels rightly raise doubts as to the wisdom of marriage. A couple's adaptability is best revealed in their handling of differences. If there seems to be a pattern to the quarrels, certain situations invariably precipitating them, it suggests basic differences as to life values, or fundamental conflicts in personality makeup.

For example, both may have strong urges to dominate, or one may be very dominating. One may be quite insecure, the quarrels resulting from the insecure person's need for reassurance, and seeking that reassurance by testing the other one beyond normal limits. Or one may be extremely selfish and thoughtless, this aspect manifesting itself in a new light when the time comes for making definite plans for marriage. Where basic differences persistently provoke a couple to quarreling, it is safe to assume that the condition would not be improved by marriage.

The question is sometimes asked: "What about dating others while one is engaged?" The author's experience is that this question is nearly always asked by an engaged person who is separated by great distance from the other, and with little prospect of being with that one for some time.

First, it is imperative that this be talked over between the two who are engaged, and agreement be reached. Such a request may reveal the instability of their engagement. A situation of this kind quite frequently points to the fact that two persons have become engaged too early. Should they have become engaged if they expect to have dates with others? I think not. Since engagement is the period of preparation for marriage, dates with others do not make up part of that preparation. Engagement is the time when two persons want to keep themselves entirely for each other, and until this is their mutual desire they should not enter into the agreements of engagement. Engagement is a testing period, true, but not for testing the partner against other dates! That belongs to courtship.

In close connection is the question of keeping former friends and sweethearts as future friends. Many are worth being kept as friends, and the best way to maintain such relations is to make them mutual. When entertained, they should be entertained by the couple. Letters should be considered by and for both husband and wife. Neither one can foster a friendship which eliminates the other. There need not be conflict or insecurity over former friends if they are mutually shared. However, if this does not seem true in any given case, then it is imperative that the former friendship be relinquished, breaking it off as constructively as possible.

Studies of Burgess and Locke and others suggest that from one-third to one-half of all engagements are broken. With early dating, increasing freedom, and with easy divorce, it is a good thing that engagement is accepted as a period of final testing in courtship. A broken engagement is better than a broken or bad marriage. This high incidence of broken engagement indicates four principles at work: (1) that young people are becoming engaged sooner than they should, and for insufficient reasons, (2) that engagement is not taken so seriously as it was formerly, (3) that young people have broader needs, are getting better acquainted during engagement, and are more realistic and free to recognize when there is little possibility of successful marriage, (4) that there is less concern, especially on the part of girls, that this may be the only chance for marriage.

Clearly, one function of engagement in our day is to eliminate from marriage those who cannot stand the experience of intimate association, and who learn this fact during an engagement which is subsequently broken. A continuation of our survey of the reasons for broken engagement brings out the following facts.

A young couple may recognize feelings of alienation arising as a result of the more intimate relationship of engagement. There may have been a high degree of happiness and a general sense of well-being when they were going together, followed by a fading of happiness when they became engaged. This general shift in feeling is sufficient to upset engagement.

It may be recognized by a couple that their engagement was decided under the pressure of friends or relatives, the pressure of campus circumstances such as mutual popularity, and the subsequent feeling that others must be right and they belong together. Engagement can be a prestige performance to meet the expectations of others.

Engagement should never be the result of a competitive social structure. Campus pressures are sometimes very great, but they must be resisted. They only make it difficult for a couple to break their engagement, causing them distressing fears and anxieties because of the probable publicity and attitudes which would arise from the very same sources that helped bring the engagement into being.

In the same way, competitive campus pressures may cause a couple to become engaged because one may fear the field and want to eliminate further competition by tying the other down to a commitment. This is as serious a mistake as an engagement made for spite.

Speaking of campus life, couples whose going steady is mostly a matter of seeing each other on campus may not have an adequate experience of seeing one another in more normal situations. Wholesome going together must include seeing each other at home, in everyday duties, in broader social groups than student gatherings. Campus dating is too often formal, and thus restricted to evening activities. In smaller colleges each date is under the spotlight. Campus prophets find delight in construing what they can whenever a fellow dates the same girl twice.

Engagement sometimes turns to sheer boredom, especially when the goal of marriage is remotely distant. The relationship suddenly begins to grow dull. One cannot hold the interest of the other. It may simply reveal that they have outgrown one another and have outlived the things that first brought them together. The relationship has just worn itself out. Kirkpatrick and Caplow, in studies of broken engagement among University of Minnesota students, found that almost half of the fellows and one-third of the girls said the reason the engagement was broken was that one or both had lost interest. Young people not only mature, but their interests and values change through experience.

If a couple get engaged because they know they will be separated in school from now on, they are expecting engagement to add a security that does not otherwise exist. This is doomed to failure. Separation is listed by Landis of the University of California as the number three cause of broken engagement. Separation will accentuate doubts and create new ones because new interests and attractions take their place. Young people in their late teens are maturing at a rapid rate, their ideas at seventeen or eighteen of an ideal mate in all likelihood changing greatly by the time they are twenty-one. Such individual maturation is often too much for engagement with separation to survive. This is especially true when one's dating life has been monopolized from the start by one person who then goes away to school.

There are immature individuals whose need for a dependency relation thrives on a relationship of going steady, even of engagement, but who break away when marriage looms close on the horizon. Inability to face responsibilities and fears of inadequacies will deter the actual consummation of that engagement in marriage.

The fears that break up engagements are complex and hidden. Given reasons for a broken engagement may not be the true reasons at all. In fact, those who are controlled by such fears may themselves be unaware of their real reasons for stopping short of marriage. It may be a fear of losing a close home relationship, or an accustomed independence. It may be the fear that one's self-esteem will be threatened by the intimacy of marriage. Some girls have been conditioned to fear sex experience or child-bearing, and so many become engaged only to try to postpone or to avoid marriage. Fears, whatever be their origin, are powerful, compulsive influences upon human behavior. Counselling will sometimes provide a way toward self-acceptance and to a transcending of fear. The counsellor is also the best one to help determine when fears make marriage unwise.

The subject of immaturity prompts the consideration of two other personality types. Often an extreme parental attachment on the side of one partner does not fully manifest itself until engagement. A girl may admire the way her fellow reverences his mother, interpreting his behavior as evidence that he will treat his wife in the same way. The assumption is doubted, however, when the son's devotion is so strong that he can see no reason why, as newly-weds, they should not live in his mother's home which is open to them. Any form of overly strong parental attachment is dangerous.

The other type of person is commonly called "a perfectionist." The person of this type will place impossible demands upon the other, and upon the other's family and friends. This is a form of unreality, a lack of adjustment to life as it is. It is quite generally a compulsive reaction to an inner insecurity. By dreaming perfection for one's imperfect self, avoiding or justifying all indications of one's own imperfection, and by contemptuously regarding others who by one's imagined self-perfection are quite inferior, one reveals a tragic need for self-acceptance. Extremely critical, easily hurt, withdrawing from problem-solving, finding little humor in the ordinary events of the day, such a one obviously takes himself too seriously and is utterly self-centered and deluded.

Engagement to such a person becomes an intolerable situation. It is always folly to hope for one-sided solutions to two-sided problems.

Many engagements do not survive contrasts in background. Cultural and social backgrounds are of major importance. The novelty of going with someone whose background is radically different is intriguing at first. Like does not always attract like. But the wider the cultural backgrounds, the less chance there is for marriage success. This is the chief difficulty with interracial marriages. It sometimes takes the period of engagement, when two young persons are getting thoroughly acquainted with future in-laws, for them to find it more and more difficult to accept the cultural backgrounds of each other.

Although a modern young person is free to marry whomever he chooses, he is influenced by what others think of his choice. During engagement, the friends and families take their new opportunity to come to know the prospective husband and wife more fully. When the partner is looked upon unfavorably by friends and family, most young people find it hard to go on with marriage. Granted, parental disapproval may not be sufficient cause for breaking up, but it is an influence not to be underestimated, for it may carry over into marriage with disruptive effects. And if a young woman recognizes that her fiancé does not seem to her friends and family to be very desirable, it not only wounds her pride but may cause her to look at his attributes more candidly herself. She may then begin to see him as others do, and decide not to go through with the marriage. Let us not lose sight of the fact that the highest ideal for an engagement and marriage blessed of God is that which includes the approval and cooperation of the parents of both young people. It should be a rare instance, and then only when a Christian counsellor can fully concur, that a parent's disapproval should be side-stepped.

Doubt is frequently given as a cause for broken engagement. It is only natural that some mixed feelings and doubts will come into the relation of engaged couples. Nevertheless, it usually comes unexpectedly in two persons in love. Women are slightly more disposed than men to doubt, perhaps relating to the fact that the woman is usually the one who is sought and won. While doubt should never be underestimated, neither should it be overestimated. Young people in the transition from adolescence to adulthood face doubts and uncertainties at all levels of their changing experience. It would be only too easy to attribute wrongly the cause of one's doubt feelings to the engagement when it might well be just the doubt that naturally accompanies a new relationship and a forthcoming responsibility.

One difficulty Christian young people should be aware of is the tendency to confuse a mutual spiritual understanding with the full-orbed love and mutuality that establishes the ground for marriage. Deep spiritual insight and understanding, the introspection that can draw two persons together quite profoundly, is no substitute for a wide range of interests, skills, and goals in marriage. Spiritual understanding and spiritual emotion are powerful forces of attraction, and together with other factors greatly enhance and complete the oneness of marriage. But there must be no substitute of spiritual oneness for the full acquaintance and adjustment which precede marriage.

Though the break of an engagement may come suddenly, it is nearly always the end of a series of disintegrating factors. At some point the disintegrating effect counterbalances and overthrows the integrating process. It is fortunate indeed when both persons conclude that the marriage will not work, and it is terminated with little difficulty. But some enagements are broken in immature and thoughtless ways. One will display a careless disregard for the feelings of the other, or even deliberately attempt to hurt the other because of one's own sense of frustration. Hurt pride all too frequently motivates the way in which the engagement is broken.

Such a break should be frankly accepted. It is unfair for one to withdraw gradually by resorting to such irregular conduct as the breaking of a date at the last minute, or the failure to return a telephone call. There is no formula for breaking engagements, but the couple so involved must handle it as constructively and thoughtfully as possible. It is the accepted ethic that the girl be permitted to announce the break, for she is the one most apt to suffer loss of status.

A wise couple will not hesitate to make the break when it is warranted. There should be no thought that such a break will ruin the other, or that the inevitable letdown is wrong. They must simply recognize that if two persons are not meeting each other's needs during engagement, it is not likely that they will find happiness together in marriage. No past pledges, no remembered intimacies, no fears of gossip nor anticipated loss of prestige should have any bearing on the decision.

The partner to whom the break may be unwelcome should wisely avoid the temptation to try to hang on. This will not bring the desired result, and it can only further disturb the ability of both of them to adjust properly. It is easy at such a time to regress to an immature level of behavior in an attempt to hold the unwilling partner. Such behavior is calculated to force the other to worry and to feel responsible for one's inability to adjust. The hurt one hopes thereby to create a new response in the loved one, and thus bring about the resumption of the engagement. The actual motivation will be, "I'm sure she would rather come back to me than to see me destroy myself." But such behavior is only concrete evidence of immaturity. These behavior patterns do not change with marriage any more than selfishness is cured by marriage. It is far better for the unwilling one to recognize that broken engagements are always broken for sufficient reasons relating to marriage happiness, and that the break should be accepted.

The extensive studies of Kirkpatrick and Caplow concerned with the length of time required to reach a normal emotional state following broken engagement are illuminating. One-third reported that the emotional trauma lasted less than one month, another third that it took from one to six months, and another third that they were not completely over it for a year or more. Further investigation revealed no significant difference between lengths of time required by men and women, and that when more time was required in any given case, it pointed to special circumstances. If one was not busy with demanding tasks, or socially in position to shift attention to a desirable substitute, longer time was needed.

Other investigators report as high as one-half indicated that the emotional adjustment was made very rapidly. Many report that the first tendency was to feel that no one else had ever endured quite the same ordeal, but this did not seem to be correlated with a serious adjustment reaction in most cases. It can be confidently said that most people seem to survive broken love affairs without any permanent ill effects, a rash of movies and novels notwithstanding.

It is difficult to convince the victim of a broken love affair that his is a typical case. Yet attaining maturity is partly learning by experience that personal recovery of emotional balance is possible from the most devastating losses or bereavements, broken engagement not excepted. Absorbing tasks can aid the process of recovery.

Students report that getting dates with others soon afterward is one of the best helps to adjustment. This is certainly healthy so long as such dating is not an attempt to "show" the other how quickly and easily one bounces back. It is healthy, too, so long as it does not lead to sudden engagement or marriage on the rebound.

It is not true that there is always a serious adjustment reaction. The most common response checked by students was that they were hurt (almost half gave this answer), but nearly one-third said that they were either indifferent or actually relieved.

There are of course those young people for whom broken engagement involves considerable personal disorganization because of the depth of the involvement. For them personality needs must now be satisfied in other ways. Emotional reactions must be dissipated and new social contacts established, often with a totally new group.

Christian young people facing engagement must seek honestly before the Lord to determine whether they have met the requirements for a sound marriage. They will not seek to force security by means of an engagement when God has given no assurance. They will put their spiritual mutuality first and foremost, but will not build their relationship on any one area of compatibility alone, even the spiritual. As the relationship is prayed about, there will be a general sense of happiness and well-being, with no major reservations or persistent doubts, and one will be free to speak to the Lord about the imminent plans with full confidence of His blessing. All areas of adjustment will be committed to Him for guidance in a most realistic way. The doubts that come from sinful and selfish motives will be dealt with before God. The counsel of a pastor will be sought. And when the announcement is made, they both will be sure they are sure!

Throughout these chapters we have been taking the measure of a cloud built for two, an exciting venture just begun. Verdant fields still lie unexplored, but it may be hoped that a sure way has been established, a high goal set forth. Christian marriage is a magnificent expression of the grace of God operative in two lives made one. The depth-dimension of such a union of persons is in their oneness in Christ—two lives unified by His indwelling life. It is a union of full personal intimacy, meeting the high cost of loving by bringing every difference to the surface that the will of God might sovereignly transcend each individual will. The love of Christ transforms that of the married lovers, giving it the divine quality of outgoingness and self-subordination. The growing experience of the forgiveness of Christ is reciprocated in the horizontal relationship of marriage, transmuting conflict into inner conquest. Even the sexual union is elevated to contribute to the sacrament of life. All liberty is limited by the Lordship of Christ to make marriage a spiritual commitment.

May it be that some of the suggested steps toward such a marriage will point the way to the true sanctity possible to dating and courtship. There are no pitfalls to be feared when life's most important relationship is three-dimensional from the earliest dating days, when Christ is the constant companion, the silent partner. The great business of our Lord is to lead each of His own to the one of His choice, and then along a successful and joyful path to that consummate day of Christian married oneness.

MORE CHALLENGING READING FROM YOUR FAVORITE AUTHORS

Complete and Unabridged

GOD'S PSYCHIATRY by Charles L. Allen   **1.50**
An actual working manual which can change your life in just seven days. From Biblical lessons come ways to banish fear, acquire confidence, and face life with new enthusiasm and peace of mind.

THE BURDEN IS LIGHT! by Eugenia Price   **1.50**
The amazing autobiography of a successful, sophisticated writer whose empty personal life was transformed when she took the Word of God literally!

A MAN CALLED PETER by Catherine Marshall   **1.25**
The glowing story of the acclaimed minister and Senate chaplain whose messages touched the heartstrings of the whole world.

PEACE WITH GOD by Billy Graham   **1.25**
Written by one of the century's most influential religious figures, here is inspiration and comfort for the man in the street.

ANGEL UNAWARE by Dale Evans Rogers   **1.25**
The poignant story of the birth, and death, of Roy and Dale Rogers' own little girl. A lasting victory over great sorrow.

THROUGH GATES OF SPLENDOR by Elisabeth Elliot   **1.25**
An on-the-scene account of the martyrdom of five American missionaries in the steaming jungles of Ecuador, an epic of unmatched courage and faith.

THE LITTLE PEOPLE by David Wilkerson   **95¢**
Conceived in hate, born without love, robbed of their childhood—these are the children of addicts and prostitutes, muggers and alcoholics. Here is their story, who they are, how they exist, and what happens to them.

ORDER FROM YOUR BOOKSTORE

If your bookstore does not stock these books, order from
SPIRE BOOKS
Box 150, Old Tappan, New Jersey 07675
Please send me the books indicated. Enclosed is my payment plus 25¢ mailing charge on first book ordered, 10¢ each additional book.

Name_____

Address_____

City_____ State_____ Zip_____

_____Amount enclosed ___Cash ___Check ___Money order (No c.o.d.'s)